# Generation Next

# Generation Next

## A Catholic Guide to
## Financial Freedom for Young Adults

Phil Lenahan

Veritas Financial Ministries

2012

## Generation Next

A Catholic Guide to Financial Freedom for Young Adults

VeritasFinancialMinistries.com

Published by Veritas Financial Ministries
P.O. Box 892425
Temecula, CA 92589-2425
www.veritasfinancialministries.com

Interior design by Russell Design
Cover design by Devin Schadt
Printed in the United States of America
ISBN: 978-0984-777006

# Contents

## A Message from Phil Lenahan

Dear Young Adult,

Life—it's an exciting thing, especially when you've got so much of it yet to live. Options and opportunities galore lie ahead of you: Will you continue your education? What work will you take up? How will you discern your true calling? Will you marry, become a priest or religious, or find fulfillment in life as a single person? Who will you, a unique human person, become?

Youth is always a time of great excitement and challenges, but our times bring a lot of drama to the table too. Consider the words Pope Benedict addressed to young people during the 2008 World Youth Day in Sydney, Australia:

> "Dear young people, let me now ask you a question. What will *you* leave to the next generation? Are you building your lives on firm foundations, building something that will endure? Are you living your lives in a way that opens up space for the Spirit in the midst of a world that wants to forget God, or even rejects him in the name of a falsely-conceived freedom? How are you using the gifts you have been given, the "power" which the Holy Spirit is even now prepared to release within you? What legacy will you leave to young people yet to come? What difference will you make?"

Your generation is called to be a light to a world full of need. This means taking up responsibility not only in the more immediately exciting areas, like getting married and starting a family, launching your career, bringing your values to bear in your political and social outreach, but also in the areas that might seem totally unromantic.

One of the biggest issues that falls into the unromantic category? Your financial life! In a way, of course, it's very interesting to you, but that's usually when you're dreaming of a Bill Gates-sized bank account, not when you're budgeting nickels and dimes for Ramen noodles until your next paycheck.

No matter what direction your life takes, one thing is certain. You can't escape entirely from the world of money. You're a physical being with physical needs, and unless you plan to loaf on your mother's couch in front of the TV for the rest of your life, the need to become smart with money will keep on popping up like an unwelcome dinner guest until you take it head on.

The good news is that you can do it! That's why I developed *Generation Next: A Personal Finance Guide for Catholic Young Adults*. Effectively managing money boils down to a few basics, and the earlier you start, the better off you'll be. Many young people make early mistakes with their finances that stay with them for a lifetime. By learning the key principles and tools now, you can avoid these mistakes and get on the road to true financial freedom.

My wife, Chelsey, and I are blessed to be the parents of seven children. It's natural for parents to want what's best for their children, and that's certainly true for us. We hope our children maintain a close relationship with the Lord throughout their lives, and experience the fulfillment that comes with that commitment. Our hope is the same for you!

*In Christ,*

Phil Lenahan

Session One

# Money and Generation Next

## Session Objectives

- Understand the importance of goal-setting: short-term thinking versus long-term thinking.

- Explain how our actions are related to our values.

- Recognize that the Church, through the Bible, Catechism, and other teachings, has important messages to share with us about money.

- Create awareness of the impact that our heritage has on who we are and how we act today.

- Make financial literacy a priority.

## Key Terms

| | | |
|---|---|---|
| Principle | Attitude | *Catechism of the Catholic Church* |
| Value | Action | Financial Literacy |
| | Bible | |

## Bible and Catechism References

John 10:10: "I came that they may have life, and have it abundantly."

Isaiah 55:8-9: "For my thoughts are not your thoughts, neither are your ways my ways, says the Lord. For as the heavens are higher than the earth, so are my ways higher than your ways and my thoughts higher than your thoughts."

John 3:16: "For God so loved the world that he gave his only Son, that whoever believes in him should not perish but have eternal life."

Catechism 27: "The desire for God is written in the human heart, because man is created by God and for God; and God never ceases to draw man to himself. Only in God will he find the truth and happiness he never stops searching for."

## Reading
## Generation Next Is You!

"A new generation has come of age, shaped by an unprecedented revolution in technology and dramatic events both at home and abroad. They are Generation Next, the cohort of young adults who have grown up with personal computers, cell phones, and the Internet and are now taking their place in a world where the only constant is rapid change."

The words and table to the right are taken from the following survey, based on the 2006 Gen Next survey data: "A Portrait of 'Generation Next': How Young People View Their Lives, Futures and Politics," January 9, 2007, conducted by the Pew Research Center For the People & the Press, a project of the Pew Research Center. In this survey, 81% of 18–25 year olds said their most important or second most important goal in life was to get rich. Coming in second was the desire for fame, and down

# Talking About My Generation's Goals

| Your generation's most important goals in life | Gen Next 18–25 | Gen X 26–40 |
|---|---|---|
| To get rich | 81% | 62% |
| To be famous | 51 | 29 |
| To help people who need help | 30 | 36 |
| To be leaders in their community | 22 | 33 |
| To become more spiritual | 10 | 31 |

Source: 2006 Gen Next Survey. Respondents were asked to choose the most important and next most important goals from these five options.

at number five, with a whopping 10%, was the goal of becoming more spiritual. When I first saw those results, I wasn't surprised that young people were focused more on money and fame than on their spirituality. After all, the need for money is pretty basic, and stepping out into the wide world to earn your living is a big deal. Faith tends to get more important as we get older—as evidenced by the responses of the 26–40 year olds. But I was surprised by the fact that money and fame were considered so much more important. And it concerns me.

What really brought home to me the fact that attitudes have undergone a titanic shift over the last few decades were the results of another survey, conducted each year by UCLA (CIRP Freshman Survey, Higher Education Research Institute). In 1967, only

42% of freshman in this survey said it was "essential" or "very important" that they be "very well off financially." But in 2005, that percentage had increased to a whopping 75%!

When asked how important it was to have a meaningful philosophy of life, a substantial majority of 86% said in 1967 that it was essential or very important. Yet that number had dwindled to only 45% in 2005. Why? It seems that our consumer-crazed culture has taken a toll on the priorities of young people.

## Setting Goals That Matter— A Higher Purpose

My oldest son has a saying that comes from his love for aviation: "Aim high." I like the passion, drive, and commitment to excellence those words convey. What does it mean to aim high when it comes to money? Jesus said, "I came that they may have life, and have it abundantly." (John 10:10) There's an attitude in today's culture that the only real kind of abundance is material; that to be really happy you need to have dollars—and lots of them. But do you? Consider the following story:

A teenage girl was sharing her hopes and dreams for the future with her parish priest. She said she wanted to do well on the college entrance exams, and the priest nodded and asked, "Then what?" She spoke of going to a prestigious college in order to get into a high-paying career. The priest nodded again and again asked, "Then what?" She told him that she was going to make a lot of money so she could buy whatever she wanted and be happy. The priest replied, "Then what?" Eventually, the wise priest's gentle probing got the teenager thinking about her later years and eventual death. He understood the words of Isaiah: "For my thoughts are not your thoughts, neither are your ways my ways, says the Lord. For as the heavens are higher than the earth, so are my ways higher than your ways and my thoughts higher than your thoughts." (Is. 55:8–9)

We tend to think of the here and now. That's natural; we're human. But our Lord has greater plans for us than just the goods of the earthly world. In the Gospel of John, we read, "For God so loved the world that he gave his only Son, that whoever believes in him should not perish but have eternal life." (John 3:16)

The Lord has created us for a great purpose: to know and love him in this world, and be with him for all eternity. As the Catechism says, "The desire for God is written in the human heart, because man is created by God and for God; and God never ceases to draw man to himself. Only in God will he find the truth and happiness he never stops searching for." (CCC 27)

Just as with the young teen, we all need to answer the "Then what?" question. When we answer it well, we will have discovered the ultimate purpose money should have in our lives. Uncovering that purpose and helping you live it out is the objective of this course.

## Success with Life Leads to Success with Money

Your success with money will depend on both attitude and financial skill. But as with many things in life, managing money well is about 80 percent attitude and 20 percent skill. Why? Because what you do with money is a reflection of what's important to you. It's a reflection of your life. And it's your attitude toward money that will determine the actions you take with it.

So what will your attitude toward money be? What values will form and shape it? Will they be the values of a consumer-crazed culture that seeks happiness in things? Or will they be the eternal values Jesus proposes to us in the Gospels and through the Church? Here is a simple diagram of how this "values hierarchy" works:

# Principles and Values
↓
# Attitude
↓
# Actions

During our lives, we make literally millions of decisions. Many of these decisions are relatively minor, such as:

○ What will I have for breakfast?

○ What should I wear today?

But many of your decisions will impact you and those around you in much bigger ways. Consider:

○ What type of work will I do?

○ Will my faith be a priority?

○ Will I be a person of honesty and integrity?

○ Who will I marry?

Money touches just about every aspect of our lives. All our decisions, both big and small, will in some way relate to money. And although it's important that good decisions be made about even minor things—as lots of small decisions can add up to a big impact, it's especially important that we get the big decisions right.

Thank the Lord he didn't leave us on our own to sort out how to make good decisions managing our money. He had a lot to say on that topic. Did you know that there are hundreds of references to money in the Bible and the *Catechism of the Catholic Church*, and that about half of the Gospel parables Jesus used to teach us involve money or material things? The references in the Bible talk about the big picture. They convey principles that, when consistently followed, lead to success with money. They deal with such questions as:

6 Who owns it all anyway?

6 Why is it important to keep God first in your life and what steps can you take to do so?

6 Why does growing in generosity help you grow in happiness?

6 Marriage and money: how do you avoid common pitfalls and build a beautiful relationship for a lifetime?

6 Why is having a financial plan so important?

6 What attitude should you have toward debt?

6 How can you save, invest, and create wealth for the future?

6 What role should wealth play in your life?

When you develop your approach to managing money based on the values and principles put forth by Jesus and his Church, you set a solid foundation that will lead you to true financial freedom. I remember the comments of one woman who went through our small group study. She said, "It's helped define our values, and from your values, you make your choices in life. I feel a much stronger sense of what my values are with money, and that's making those choices easier." She's on to something!

## Our Past Influences Our Future— The Heritage Question

Nothing does more for the direction of your future than the commitment to develop a strong relationship with the Lord. At the same time, it's important to recognize that our past also powerfully affects our future. So it's good to think about where we come from.

In my travels giving seminars, I ask attendees to consider what I call the "heritage question." Participants look back at their parents' attitude toward money— how they managed it and communicated about it, and how that has influenced the participants' approach to money today. In my experience, this has been a fun and enlightening process.

When I answer the heritage question, I especially think of how my dad's story has influenced me. My dad grew up on a farm in northern California during the Great Depression. Like many others, he remembered his parents struggling just to provide the basics. Multiple families lived on the property so they could share expenses, and the older children were expected to work in order to help make ends meet.

One of the unusual things about my dad was that he didn't like summer fruits. Mom and we kids enjoyed peaches, nectarines, cherries, plums, and all the other fruits that come with summer, but dad just wouldn't partake, even if the delectable fruit was inside a delicious pie!

His distaste for summer fruit only made sense after he shared his

Depression-era story. You see, the job he had as a teen was picking fruit in the nearby orchards, and on many days fruit was his breakfast, lunch, and dinner. Given that, his distaste for summer fruit later in life made all the sense in the world. Isn't it interesting how our past shapes our future?

Dad went on to fight in the army during World War II, married my mom upon his return, became a CPA, and raised a family of five children. He was a gentle and down-to-earth man. We lived in a comfortable home in a typical middle-class neighborhood. In his later years, he shared with me that over the years he and mom wondered whether they should have moved "up the hill" to the more expensive part of town. That they chose not to do so was a reminder to me of their simple approach to life.

I don't remember mom and dad talking a lot about money—at least in front of us kids. But I do know they were responsible with their resources and sacrificed for things they believed in, including sending all five kids through Catholic school.

As I travel around the country and hear people's stories, it's very common for those raised by parents who lived through the Great Depression and World War II to have had imbued in them a sense of duty, an understanding of the value of a dollar, a strong work ethic, and a belief in sacrificing for a greater cause. People often answer the heritage question by saying that they didn't have much money growing up, but they didn't know any different. They just knew their needs were met and that they were loved.

Of course, just as there are dysfunctional families today, so there were in prior generations. Many who lived through the Great Depression developed an unhealthy attachment to things.

They became hoarders, often of things with no apparent value. Sometimes they are known as "pack rats." What do you think fills all the rental storage units you see around town!

All our heritages come with a mix of positives and negatives. What's important is the heritage we leave for our children and grandchildren, and ultimately that's up to you. The Lord has promised we won't be alone on this journey. He wants to be with us along the way. We just need to invite him to be a part of our lives, and to be guided by his teachings and by the Church.

## The Importance of Financial Literacy

I noted earlier that attitude represents 80 percent of the reason you'll succeed with money, but there's still that remaining 20 percent that relates to knowledge and skill. Unglamorous as it may at first seem, it's a 20 percent you don't want to skip over!

# Take a few minutes to answer the heritage question yourself!

| Answering The Heritage Question |
| --- |
| What is your parents' attitude toward money? |
| How do they communicate about money? |
| How do they manage their money? |
| How has all the above influenced how you think about and manage your money today? |

# Money Stats

| 93% of American parents with teens worry their teens might make financial missteps such as: | Overspending or living beyond their means **(67%)** |
| --- | --- |
| | Getting in over their head with credit card debt **(65%)** |
| | Failing to save for emergencies **(60%)** |
| | Failing to stick to a budget **(57%)** |
| | A full third of parents **(33%)** anticipate their "golden years" will likely involve helping their kids financially. |

Source: Charles Schwab, Schwab "Parents & Money" Survey: March 26, 2008

When I speak or answer questions on the radio, I am always surprised at the general population's lack of financial knowledge. Young people are graduating from high school and college without awareness of even the most basic financial concepts.

In 2008, the President's Advisory Council on Financial Literacy was established. As part of its work, the Council instituted a 35-question exam on personal finance issues. The average score? 56%! That's not a healthy indicator for the financial future of most Americans, nor for the culture at large. Take this opportunity to learn about financial management enlightened by your faith. The two are a powerful combination that will serve you well over the years.

Over the next several sessions, you're going to learn the basic things you need to know about how to manage money effectively, including:

- ⦿ What does it mean to have a financial plan?

- ⦿ What role should giving play in your financial life?

- ⦿ How can you effectively manage your banking relationships?

- ⦿ What does the Bible say about saving? How can you know how much you should save for the future?

- ⦿ What does the Bible say about debt? What is the difference between productive and unproductive debt?

- ⦿ What are credit scores and credit reports, and how do they affect you?

- ⦿ What role should insurance play in your financial life?

- ⦿ What is the key to creating wealth?

- ⦿ What does the Bible say about wealth, and the responsibilities that come with it?

- ⦿ How can you be a savvy consumer and stretch the resources you have?

It may seem like a lot to take in all at once, but the good news is that you don't have to. We'll cover each of these areas as we work through the program together. With each session, you'll learn building blocks that, when put together, will provide a solid foundation for a bright financial future. Whatever your current level of financial smarts may be, those words—"bright financial future"—are directed at you.

## Discussion Topics

Read the discussion topic questions and write down your thoughts. This should be done prior to your class or small group get-together. In your class or small group, you'll share your thoughts with each other. For those discussion topics that list a Bible or Catechism reference, review it by referring to the applicable text at the beginning of the session.

## Discussion Topic 1
## Isaiah 55:8-9

How do you determine what you'll spend money on? What role do your parents play in setting those priorities? Your friends? The media—including TV, Internet, and magazines? Does your relationship with the Lord influence how you spend money? Should it?

_____

_____

_____

_____

_____

_____

_____

_____

_____

## Discussion Topic 2

Think of the person you most admire in terms of his or her attitude toward money and how he or she manages/managed the resources he or she has/had. This may be a person in your life today, someone in today's broader culture, or a person in history. Describe why you admire him or her.

_____

_____

_____

_____

_____

_____

_____

_____

_____

_____

## Activity

Follow the instructions of your teacher/leader as he (or she) guides you through this session's activity. The activity is designed to help you apply the concepts learned in this session in a fun and engaging way.

## Session Two

# Money and Society

## Session Objectives

᧝ Understand how government fiscal policies and monetary policies interact with personal finances.

᧝ Recognize how economic cycles have occurred through history and how they impact personal finances.

᧝ Learn the foundational social teachings of the Church on socialization and subsidiarity.

## Key Terms

| | | |
|---|---|---|
| Bartering | Currency | Inflation |
| Deflation | Hyperinflation | Federal Reserve System |
| Gross Domestic Product | Taxes | Liquidity |
| Recession | Depression | Unemployment rate |

Socialization                    Subsidiarity

*Rerum Novarum*: On the Condition of the Working Classes

*Centesimus Annus*: On the Hundredth Anniversary of Rerum Novarum

*Caritas in Veritate*: Charity in Truth

## Bible and Catechism References

Genesis 1: 27-28: "So God created man in his own image, in the image of God he created him; male and female he created them. And God blessed them, and God said to them, "Be fruitful and multiply, and fill the earth and subdue it; and have dominion over the fish of the sea and over the birds of the air and over every living thing that moves upon the earth.""

Catechism 373: "In God's plan man and woman have the vocation of 'subduing' the earth as stewards of God. This sovereignty is not to be an arbitrary and destructive domination. God calls man and woman, made in the image of the Creator 'who loves everything that exists,' to share in his providence toward other creatures; hence their responsibility for the world God has entrusted to them."

Catechism 2426: "The development of economic activity and growth in production are meant to provide for the needs of human beings. Economic life is not meant solely to multiply goods produced and increase profit or power; it is ordered first of all to the service of persons, of the whole man, and of the entire human community.

Economic activity, conducted according to its own proper methods, is to be exercised within the limits of the moral order, in keeping with social justice so as to correspond to God's plan for man."

Catechism 2424: "A theory that makes profit the exclusive norm and ultimate end of economic activity is morally unacceptable. The disordered desire for money cannot but produce perverse effects."

Catechism 2425: "'. . . there are many human needs which cannot be satisfied by the market.' Reasonable regulation of the marketplace and economic initiatives, in keeping with a just hierarchy of values and a view to the common good, is to be commended."

Catechism 1883: "Excessive intervention by the state can threaten personal freedom and initiative. The teaching of the Church has elaborated the principle of subsidiarity, according to which 'a community of higher order should not interfere in the internal life of a community of a lower order, depriving the latter of its functions, but rather should support it in case of need and help to co-ordinate its activity with the activities of the rest of society, always with a view to the common good.'"

## Reading

This is a personal finance program, not an advanced economics class, but in order to understand how to manage your money, you need to understand a few things about the bigger picture of how money functions in society.

## The Banking System and National Currency

Money is such an everyday part of our lives that we take its use for granted. When we want something at the store, it doesn't even cross our minds as we approach the checkout counter that the store may not accept the dollars (or credit or debit cards) in our purse or wallet as payment. But it hasn't always been this easy.

Think about what it would be like to buy an orange if you didn't have any money. What could you offer the seller in return for the orange? If you had some extra tomato seeds, would the seller exchange the orange for the seeds? Maybe, especially if he liked tomatoes. This is called bartering. It's how people first traded for things they wanted.

Bartering has not completely died out as a method of trading, but it's easy to see its limits. What if the person with the orange doesn't like tomatoes? Unless he knows he can easily trade the tomato seeds for something else he wants, he's probably out of luck.

Over the centuries, monetary systems and currencies have developed and been refined to make it easier for people to trade things of value. So instead of tomato seeds, you are able to offer a dollar for the orange. Now the seller has flexibility to use that dollar to buy whatever he chooses. He isn't forced to find someone who will accept tomato seeds for what he wants to buy. That just made his life a whole lot easier.

So what is this thing called currency? It's "something (as coins, treasury notes, and banknotes) that is in circulation as a medium of exchange," according to Merriam-Webster's Dictionary. Currency facilitates trading. For our purposes, we'll use the term "money" interchangeably with "currency."

## Currency and Trust of the People

When it comes to money, trust is incredibly important. People need to have confidence that the money they have today will hold its value over time. Businesses making

long-term commitments need that same confidence. There are many times in world history when those in charge of managing the money supply have, through either poor judgment or outright abuse, made decisions that have led to either inflation or deflation. Inflation is when there is a general rise in the price of goods over time. Deflation is when the price of goods declines over time.

While a little inflation is manageable, hyperinflation is when money loses its value very rapidly, for example, when the cost of an item doubles in price every day. Hyperinflation occurs when there is a loss of confidence in the currency. This normally occurs when money is printed at a much faster rate than the economy is growing. This causes more dollars to chase after fewer goods. When that happens, prices rise.

In the United States, hyperinflation of "Continental" currency occurred during the Revolutionary War and of "Confederate" currency during the Civil War. Although the country has weathered bouts of regular inflation in the years since, we've been fortunate not to have experienced hyperinflation. It has, though, wreaked havoc upon the economies of many other countries, including Germany after World War I and more recently Zimbabwe. Hyperinflation often leads to serious social unrest. While deflation, a general decline in the price of goods, may seem at first like a good thing, its economic repercussions, although opposite those of hyperinflation, are just as serious. When deflation occurs, people hoard their money as they wait for prices to reach bottom. This results in a downward spiral of economic activity, and often leads to high unemployment and, again, social unrest.

Because the consequences of substantial inflation or deflation are so devastating, one of the important roles of government is to provide a stable currency for its citizens. In the United States, that responsibility has been given to the Federal Reserve System, the central banking system of the United States.

## The National Economy and You

How do these money concepts affect the United States economy and, more specifically, your personal cash? First, how big do you think the U.S. economy is? Gross Domestic Product (GDP) is a frequently cited statistic that reflects the total value of goods and services produced by a nation over the course of a year. Today, the United States' gross domestic product is a whopping $14 trillion! Picture this: If you stacked $14 trillion worth of one dollar bills on top of each other, the stack would reach 952,000 miles into space—about the same distance that the earth is from the sun.

Another important number is the portion of gross domestic product spent to support federal, state, and local governments. In the accompanying table, you can see a history of this relationship at the federal level going back to the early 1900's. Over the last several years, it's been close to 20 percent, and more recently has climbed into the mid-20 percent range. You can see that the percentage has grown steadily over the years as the federal government has taken

# History of United States GDP and Federal Spending

| Year | GDP (In Billions of Dollars) | Federal Spending as % of GDP |
|------|------------------------------|------------------------------|
| 1930 | 97.4 | 3.4 |
| 1935 | 69.6 | 9.2 |
| 1940 | 96.8 | 9.8 |
| 1945 | 221.4 | 41.9 |
| 1950 | 273.2 | 15.6 |
| 1955 | 395.9 | 17.3 |
| 1960 | 518.9 | 17.8 |
| 1965 | 687.5 | 17.2 |
| 1970 | 1,012.9 | 19.3 |
| 1975 | 1,560.8 | 21.3 |
| 1980 | 2,725.4 | 21.7 |
| 1985 | 4,148.9 | 22.8 |
| 1990 | 5,737.0 | 21.8 |
| 1995 | 7,325.1 | 20.7 |
| 2000 | 9,708.4 | 18.4 |
| 2005 | 12,234.9 | 20.2 |
| 2010 | 14,728.8 | 24.4 |

Source: Whitehouse.gov

on a more substantial social role. The percentage also increases dramatically during wartime as a result of the spike in spending to fund the wars.

It's interesting to note how the level of government spending in the United States compares to other economically advanced countries, especially those of Western Europe. You can see a few of those relationships in the accompanying chart.

Historically, federal spending in the United States has been substantially less as a percentage of GDP than that of other Western European countries. This reflects the longtime tendency of Americans, as an independent-minded people, to focus on local solutions to issues.

To the extent that government's role increases, it must tax citizens at a higher level to meet those obligations. Taxes come in many forms, including taxes on corporate and personal income, energy, estates, retail sales, property, and many other things. In order to keep the economy healthy, taxes need to remain low enough to give citizens the incentive to be productive while still being adequate to fund the responsibilities the government has taken on. Much of politics is about striking a balance between those who want government to play a smaller role and those who want it to shoulder greater responsibilities.

## Economic Cycles

Throughout history, the U.S. economy has experienced what is commonly called the business

# Government Spending as a Percent of GDP

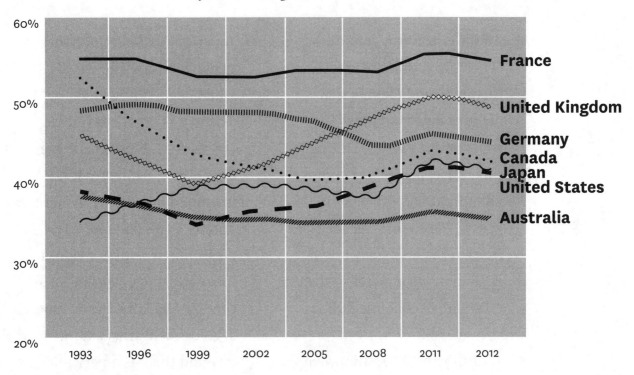

Source: OECD Economic Outlook, Volume 2011 Issue 1 - No. 89 - © OECD 2011

or economic cycle. It's essential that you are aware of this because you'll have to navigate your finances both in times of economic expansion and of economic decline. The actions you take during such times will significantly impact how well you succeed with money over the long run.

Although economic cycles repeat over time and exhibit similar characteristics, they vary in length and intensity. Economic cycles include:

⚬ **Periods of expansion**, which are typically accompanied by low interest rates that encourage the use of debt to fund economic activity.

○ As the expansion continues, economic activity reaches **unsustainable levels** that often lead to **"bubbles" in investment values**. During this phase, people's emotions are upbeat and there is a general sense that the good times won't end. Easy credit is often a major factor in the creation of economic bubbles.

○ A turning point occurs when the **bubble bursts**, which often triggers other crises in the economic and financial system. Often this phase is accompanied by a contraction in the availability of credit owing to high interest rates, lack of liquidity, or a simple unwillingness to lend resulting from a concern that borrowers aren't financially healthy enough to repay their loans.

○ A period of **slower economic growth or decline** ensues, which, depending on its severity, is characterized as stagnation, recession, or even depression. An increasing unemployment rate, business and banking failures, and declining investment values mark this stage. During such times, especially during more severe downturns, emotions are raw and there is a pervading sense of doom and gloom.

○ Finally, after the excesses have been purged from the economy, the cycle turns to the **recovery** phase and activity resumes at a more normal level.

When it comes to personal finances, people often make decisions based on their emotions. You can easily see how that can lead to poor decision making. Just as prices of investments (take your pick: stocks, bonds, real estate, commodities) reach their highs, it seems to people that the good times will never end. They don't want to miss the ride, and they make commitments they can't afford, often funding investments through borrowing.

When asset values decline, they end up owing more than they own. At the opposite end of the cycle (when things look like gloom and doom), people decide they just can't take the bad news any more, and they decide to sell their investments at a substantial loss, forgetting that the start of a recovery is just around the corner. They frequently miss the initial (and often substantial) recovery in asset values when it finally arrives. When we make investing decisions based on emotions, we tend to buy high and sell low—not a recipe for success.

## Economics and the Church

The Church doesn't participate directly in politics or in the running of a nation's economy (other than Vatican City State), but it does propose principles that will lead to healthier societies if nations follow them. These principles are represented by Jesus Christ and his Gospel teachings, which include:

6 Promoting an economic system that has the dignity of man as its primary objective:

"The development of economic activity and growth in production are meant to provide for the needs of human beings. Economic life is not meant solely to multiply goods produced and increase profit or power; it is ordered first of all to the service of persons, of the whole man, and of the entire human community. Economic activity, conducted according to its own proper methods, is to be exercised within the limits of the moral order, in keeping with social justice so as to correspond to God's plan for man." (CCC 2426)

◌ An understanding of the need for profit and efficiency, without making profit the "ultimate end of economic activity," because "the disordered desire for money cannot but produce perverse effects." (CCC 2424)

In applying these two principles, the Church rejects both communism and socialism, because these systems are associated with atheism and totalitarianism. It is interesting to note that the Church also does not accept a "pure" form of capitalism, in which the economy is regulated solely by the law of the marketplace. ". . . [T]here are many human needs which cannot be satisfied by the market. Reasonable regulation of the marketplace and economic initiatives, in keeping with a just hierarchy of values and a view to the common good, is to be commended." (CCC 2425)

## The Principles of Socialization and Subsidiarity

It is important here to discuss two additional principles: socialization and subsidiarity. Socialization isn't the same as socialism. Socialism refers to public or state ownership of the means of production, and as noted above, the Church has rejected it as a viable economic system. Socialization, on the other hand, recognizes that man doesn't live alone on an island, but instead is part of a broader society with the need to interact with that society in multiple ways.

Think for a moment about the types of interactions you have: with family, friends, school, work, or clubs you belong to, buying things from businesses, getting your driving license from the state—the list could go on and on. At its best, socialization helps you attain worthy objectives that exceed your individual capacity to do so. (CCC 1882)

Socialization can be a very good thing, but the Church notes that it also presents dangers. "Excessive intervention by the state can threaten personal freedom and initiative." (CCC 1883) In order to minimize this danger, the Church encourages people first to look to the smallest and least centralized forms of community as they seek solutions for the issues of the day. This is known as the principle of subsidiarity, and is described as follows:

"A community of higher order should not interfere in the internal life of a community of a lower order, depriving the latter of its functions, but rather should support it in case of need and help to co-ordinate its activity with the activities of the rest of society, always with a view to the common good." (CCC 1883)

Generally speaking, solving problems locally makes sense, while recognizing at the same time that some issues require solutions at the state, national, or even international level.

The writings of several popes have been especially influential when it comes to how gospel values should apply in the economic realm. These include *Rerum Novarum: On the Condition of the Working Classes* by Pope Leo XIII, which was issued in 1891. He wrote it as a response to the emerging threat of communism, so although it covers many issues, one of its focuses is the establishment of the right to private property. In 1991, Pope John Paul II issued *Centesimus Annus: On the Hundredth Anniversary of Rerum Novarum* after the historic fall of the Berlin Wall in 1989. More recently, Pope Benedict issued *Caritas in Veritate: Charity in Truth,* which included guidance related to the financial crisis of 2008–2009. A little time spent with these encyclicals will reward you with a deeper appreciation of how much the economic system matters to a person's ability to live as God intended him to live.

## Summary

You don't manage your money in a vacuum. Like it or not, you depend on the vitality of the nation's economy and the economic systems that man has developed over the centuries. Understanding those systems better will help you thrive in your financial future.

## Discussion Topics

Read the discussion topic questions and write down your thoughts. This should be done prior to your class or small group get-together. In your class or small group, you'll share your thoughts with each other. For those discussion topics that list a Bible or Catechism reference, review it by referring to the applicable text at the beginning of the session.

## Discussion Topic 1
## Genesis 1: 27–28, Catechism 373

What does it mean for men and women to have dominion over the earth? How should men and women being made in the image of God guide them in acting out this dominion?

_____

_____

_____

_____

_____

_____

_____

_____

_____

## Discussion Topic 2

Make a list of key words that describe what a healthy and just economic system should look like.

_____

_____

_____

_____

_____

_____

_____

_____

_____

_____

## Activity

Follow the instructions of your teacher/leader as he (or she) guides you through this session's activity. The activity is designed to help you apply the concepts learned in this session in a fun and engaging way.

## Session Three

# God, Money, and You

## Session Objectives

○ Understand the difference between God's role with money and our role with money as described in sacred Scripture.

○ Recognize that each of us is called to grow in virtue. Be able to relate the call to virtue to how we manage our money.

○ Assess your general personality type and be able to relate that to your money personality type.

## Key Terms

| | | |
|---|---|---|
| Creator | Owner | Manager |
| Steward of Providence | Holiness (Call to holiness) | Virtues |
| Vices | Capital Sins | Spiritual Plan |

## Bible and Catechism References

Psalm 24:1: "The earth is the Lord's and the fulness thereof, the world and those who dwell therein; for he has founded it upon the seas, and established it upon the rivers."

Catechism 2404: "In his use of things man should regard the external goods he legitimately owns not merely exclusive to himself but common to others also, in the sense that they can benefit others as well as himself. The ownership of any property makes its holder a steward of Providence, with the task of making it fruitful and communicating its benefit to others, first of all his family."

Timothy 6:9–10: "But those who desire to be rich fall into temptation, into a snare, into many senseless and hurtful desires that plunge men into ruin and destruction. For the *love of money* [emphasis mine] is the root of all evils; it is through this craving that some have wandered away from the faith and pierced their hearts with many pangs."

Catechism 2013: "All Christians in any state or walk of life are called to the fullness of Christian life and to the perfection of charity. All are called to holiness: 'Be perfect, as your heavenly Father is perfect.'"

Philippians 4:8: "Finally, brethren, whatever is true, whatever is honorable, whatever is just, whatever is pure, whatever is lovely, whatever is gracious, if there is any excellence, if there is anything worthy of praise, think about these things."

Romans 7:15: "I do not understand my own actions. For I do not do what I want, but I do the very thing I hate."

Matthew 7:24–27: "'Every one then who hears these words of mine and does them will be like a wise man who built his house upon the rock; and the rain fell, and the floods came, and the winds blew and beat upon that house, but it did not fall, because it had been founded on the rock. And every one who hears these words of mine and does not do them will be like a foolish man who built his house upon the sand; and the rain fell, and the floods came, and the winds blew and beat against that house; and it fell; and great was the fall of it."

1 Timothy 4:7–8: "Train yourself in godliness; for while bodily training is of some value, godliness is of value in every way, as it holds promise for the present life and also for the life to come."

# Reading

This is one of the most important sessions in this program. Why? Because how you manage your money will be influenced primarily by your behavior. If your behavior is right, the rest of the pieces will fall into place.

A young man graduated from college with great career ambition. He kept his nose to the grindstone, and focused on making his mark and getting ahead. He succeeded at climbing the corporate ladder one rung at a time. Over the years, though, he made no time for God. His wife and children drifted away from him. Personal relationships lost their importance to him. Even his wife's filing for divorce didn't stop him. Eventually, he reached the top of the ladder, and it finally hit him. He realized he had climbed the wrong ladder.

This story plays itself out in a variety of circumstances in thousands of families every year. What can we take from it? It's not that we don't need to concern ourselves with developing a strong work ethic and succeeding in our career. We do. But the Lord calls us to excellence in all things. It is a matter of priorities and balance. We want to make sure we are climbing the right ladder!

Money, career, possessions—all of these are part of our lives. But they aren't our reason for being. We exist to grow in knowledge and love of the Lord in this life, to be with him forever in the next, and to bring God's love to those within our sphere of influence— our spouse, children, relatives, friends, classmates, co-workers, and the less fortunate.

In Session One, I broadly touched on how the values of our faith should influence our attitude toward money and how we manage it. In this session, you'll see that this is very personal. It's about you and your personal relationship with Jesus Christ.

Once you understand how the relationship between God, money, and you works, you'll be in a position to learn and apply practical money management skills in a way that harmonizes with your faith.

## God's Role and Our Role

Let's start at the beginning by discovering God's role and the role that he has given us when it comes to money and material things. Psalm 24:1 says, "The earth is the Lord's and the fulness thereof, the world and those who dwell therein; for he has founded it upon the seas, and established it upon the rivers." This is just one example in which the Bible describes God's role as creator and owner. There are several others.

It's pretty easy to think of God as Creator, but we tend to think of ourselves as owners, don't we? Is that how God thinks of us? What role has he given us? It's described in the Catechism this way:

"In his use of things, man should regard the external goods he legitimately owns not merely exclusive to himself, but common to others also, in the sense that they can benefit others as well as himself. The ownership of any property makes its holder a steward of Providence, with the task of making it fruitful and communicating its benefit to others, first of all his family." (CCC 2404)

We are described as stewards of Providence. What is a steward? "One employed in a large household or estate to manage domestic concerns," according to Merriam-Webster's Dictionary. The dictionary also uses the word "manager" to describe a steward. God has entrusted to each of us many gifts, along with the opportunity to use them in ways that please him. These gifts include money and possessions, but also our time and talent, our intellect and emotions, our physical being, our sexuality—our whole person.

How do we reconcile the fact that Catechism 2404 describes us as stewards and owners in the same section? It's simple. For society to function in an orderly manner, we need to have "temporal" or temporary ownership of physical goods. That's why Pope Leo XIII wrote of the right to private property in *Rerum Novarum*. Yet, the hard fact is that we won't be taking anything with us when we die. As a good friend of mine says, "We are owners before men and stewards before God."

Why am I sweating this distinction between being an owner and a steward? Because it makes all the difference in how you'll view your responsibility with money. I remember visiting with one married couple, who shared their story with me. They used to argue a lot about money— you know, the whole his versus hers thing. Once they recognized their eternal role as a steward of the Lord, the arguments came to a halt. As they said, "How can you fight about something that's not even yours?"

When you understand and embrace your role as a steward of Providence, you can have confidence that you are climbing the right ladder.

## Money: Good or Evil?

I was once a guest on a Catholic television program. The host opened the interview by asking, "Phil, didn't St. Paul say that money is the root of all evil?" Since it was live TV, I was glad I knew the reference the priest had in mind. (The priest, of course, was just having a little fun with me and the audience.) The reference was to St. Paul's first letter to Timothy.

> "But those who desire to be rich fall into temptation, into a snare, into many senseless and hurtful desires that plunge men into ruin and destruction. For the *love of money* [emphasis mine] is the root of all evils; it is through this craving that some have wandered away from the faith and pierced their hearts with many pangs." (1 Tim. 6:9-10)

If the love of money is the root of all evil, then money isn't good or evil in itself. As an inanimate object, it can't be. What makes it good or bad for us is our attitude toward it and what we do with it. But keeping our attitude toward money healthy from God's perspective isn't easy. Pope Benedict once said, "Money is not 'dishonest' in itself, but more than anything else, it can close man in a blind egocentrism." Read that quote again. *More than anything else.* Powerful words, coming from the pope. So while money isn't evil in itself, the Lord makes it abundantly clear that we need to put it in its proper place.

## The Call to Holiness: Becoming a Steward of Providence

Christ wants us to get our priorities straight. He wants us to order our lives according to the goal he's set for us as human beings—with the ultimate goal of sharing eternal life with him. That's really what life boils down to. It means embracing the gift of sanctifying grace received at baptism and choosing to love God each day of our lives in order to keep that grace alive and active in our souls. As the Catechism says, "Sanctifying grace makes us 'pleasing to God.'" (CCC 2024)

So the surprising reality is this: Being a steward of Providence is a key part of the call to holiness, the call to pursue our ultimate goal. The Catechism describes the call to holiness this way:

"All Christians in any state or walk of life are called to the fullness of Christian life and to the perfection of charity. All are called to holiness: 'Be perfect, as your heavenly Father is perfect.'" (CCC 2013)

## Obstacles and Opportunities

A priest friend of mine says, "Phil, we are stewards whether we like it or not. The question is: What kind of stewards are we going to be?" Will we want and choose to make decisions that are pleasing to God or not? Another way of asking this is: Will we choose to live our life in a virtuous way? What, then, is a virtue exactly? The Catechism describes a virtue as "an habitual and firm disposition to do the good." (1803) Vices, or capital sins, oppose the virtues.

What does a course on personal finance have to do with virtues and vices? Just this: As I noted earlier, succeeding in life with money is about 20 percent skill and 80 percent behavior, and that behavior is a function of virtues and vices. Is it easy for us to always choose to do the good? If only it were. Because of our fallen nature and original sin, it's an effort for us to do what's right—especially to be consistent about it.

Even St. Paul who reached great heights, struggled with this. He speaks eloquently of the virtues in Philippians 4:8: "Finally, brethren, whatever is true, whatever is honorable, whatever is just, whatever is pure, whatever is lovely, whatever is gracious, if there is any excellence, if there is anything worthy of praise, think about these things." Yet in Romans 7:15 the same St. Paul wrote, "I do not understand my own actions. For I do not do what I want, but I do the very thing I hate."

We can each relate to the inner struggle between the virtues and the vices. It's common for each of us to be shining examples of one or two virtues, and to fall prey to one or two predominant vices in our lives. These are our natural tendencies.

# Virtues

| | | |
|---|---|---|
| Faith | Hope | Charity |
| Prudence | Justice | Fortitude |
| Temperance | Joy | Peace |
| Mercy | Generosity | Wisdom |
| Understanding | Counsel | Knowledge |
| Piety | Fear of the Lord | Patience |
| Kindness | Goodness | Gentleness |
| Modesty | Self-control | Chastity |
| Faithfulness | | |

# Vices

| | | |
|---|---|---|
| Pride | Avarice | Envy |
| Wrath | Lust | Gluttony |
| Sloth | | |

Here are lists of virtues and vices. We've provided definitions in the Appendix. Take a few minutes to reflect on them. Which virtues are your greatest strengths? What vices do you have to fight the most?

## Personality Types

Economic activity is human activity. It's not some mystery miracle science. So when Socrates said, "Know thyself" centuries ago, he uttered words that apply every bit as much to young people in the twenty-first century as to the old Greek geezers listening to him back then. You need to figure out what's getting you where you are, and what you need to change to get where you want to go.

Personality tests are tools that help you understand what makes you tick. They help you learn which virtues are likely to be your biggest strengths, and which vices will be your biggest obstacles. You can use that knowledge to grow in the virtues and lessen the destructive influence that vices play in your life.

Ever since Plato came up with the four temperaments—melancholic, choleric, phlegmatic, and sanguine—personality typing has been a popular and often immensely useful practice. Different systems and variations exist, but they all boil down to four basic types. You can easily find a good free test online. Some of the best ones are at www.keirsey.com and www.humanmetrics.com.

By taking one of these tests, you will learn which of the four major personality types best describes your tendencies. Bear in mind that each type has both good qualities

and shortcomings, and that most people are in fact a combination of types. There's no need to worry about the outcome. Just have fun with the test. There is no right answer. Be as honest with yourself as you can. Once you have your results, think about your natural tendencies in light of the virtues and vices and how they affect your money choices.

If you're an idealist (that is, if that's your dominant side), for example, you clearly see the potential for good in the world. Let's say you have the virtue of great faith, and are dreaming big about building a home for teen moms. Your vision and drive are your strengths, but your weaknesses or vices might be impatience and impracticality about actually getting things done. In your haste to see the result, you might sign a lease without noticing the big expenses hidden in the fine print. But if you're aware of your tendency to haste and recognize it as a danger, you can do something about it. You can strive for virtue, which always lies in balance. So, self-knowledge is vital to both your spiritual life and your pocketbook. If you don't know your weak areas, how can you strive to strengthen them?

In addition to the universally used personality types, I've developed what I call "Money Personality Types." These link personalities to particular virtues and vices that relate to money. Consider which one(s) most fit your personality. As with your general personality type, knowing your tendencies allows you to emphasize your strengths and minimize your weaknesses.

## Money Personality Types

- Prudent Paul

- Temperate Tom

- Just Jerry

- Charitable Chuck

- People Person Paula

- Sam the Slob

- Suzy Spender

- Harry the Hoarder

- Wilbert the Winner

Thank the Lord that he's given the world such a variety of personalities. That's part of what makes it such a fascinating place! Personality types may provide a general sense of what makes us tick as people, but it's still true that each of us is a unique person loved by God. Through our life's journey, he wants us to grow the positive natural traits we have (the virtues), and he wants us to minimize the weak spots (the vices). How can we make progress in growing the virtues and overcoming the vices?

## Responding to God's Call

It's one thing to know that our goal is to become more like Christ. It's quite another to live it. This is where the gifts Christ gives us through his Church become so important.

In the Gospel of Matthew 7:24–27, Jesus says: "Everyone then who hears these words of mine and does them will be like a wise man who built his house upon the rock; and the rain fell, and the floods came, and the winds blew and beat upon that house, but it did not fall, because it had been founded on the rock. And everyone who hears these words of mine and does not do them will be like a foolish man who built his house upon the sand; and the rain fell, and the floods came, and the winds blew and beat against that house; and it fell; and great was the fall of it."

Christ seeks us out, proposing to each one of us a new way of life, a life rooted in his life. When we accept his proposal, we want to grow closer and closer to him, and this means growing in grace. The channels of grace Christ gave us are the sacraments, especially the ongoing sacraments of the Eucharist and reconciliation.

## The Importance of Exercise

Each of us knows how important it is to make physical exercise a part of our day if we want to have healthy bodies. That morning run is supposed to tone muscles, increase blood flow, and stimulate brain activity for a brighter, better you. But a human person is body and soul, so the health of the person depends on his bodily and spiritual state. St. Paul speaks of the importance of exercising on the spiritual front if we are to have strong souls (1 Tim. 4:7–8). One way of doing this is to have a daily spiritual plan.

Start your day with a few minutes of prayer and reading. Read a page of the Bible or other Church writings. Find biographies of the saints and study their personalities. They are concrete examples that what Christ proposes is possible. Even ten or fifteen minutes doing this in the morning and evening will help you stay close to Christ. Mary points the way to her son; learn to pray the rosary. Attend Mass and receive communion as often as you can. Make regular confession.

Christ wants to be close to you. He is knocking at the door of your heart. Only you can open it. You do so by seeking him through the gifts he has entrusted to his Church, the gifts of the sacraments. If you open yourself to them, you will become the steward of Providence God wants you to be.

## Discussion Topics

Read the discussion topic questions and write down your thoughts. This should be done prior to your class or small group get-together. In your class or small group, you'll share your thoughts with each other. For those discussion topics that list a Bible or Catechism reference, review it by referring to the applicable text at the beginning of the session.

## Discussion Topic 1
## Catechism 2404

Discuss the differences between being an owner and a steward. How should being a steward of Providence influence how you think about money and what you do with it?

_____

_____

_____

_____

_____

_____

_____

_____

_____

## Discussion Topic 2

Discuss the strengths and weaknesses of at least one "Money Personality Type." Then write down five ways in which the strengths of that personality type help one be a steward of Providence, and five ways in which the weaknesses of that personality type may be an obstacle to being a steward of Providence.

_____

_____

_____

_____

_____

_____

_____

_____

_____

## Activity

Follow the instructions of your teacher/leader as he (or she) guides you through this session's activity. The activity is designed to help you apply the concepts learned in this session in a fun and engaging way.

## Session Four

# Financial Planning 101

## Session Objectives

𝒪 Realize the important role financial planning has in succeeding with money management.

𝒪 Understand how to use a balance sheet and budget.

𝒪 Learn how to manage your checkbook.

## Key Terms

| | | |
|---|---|---|
| Balance Sheet | Asset | Liability |
| Net Worth | Budget | Income |
| Expense | NSF (Not Sufficient Funds) | Bank Reconciliation |

## Bible and Catechism References

Tobit 4:19: "Bless the Lord God on every occasion; ask him that your ways may be made straight and that all your paths and plans may prosper."

Proverbs 27:23: "Know well the condition of your flocks, and give attention to your herds."

Proverbs 21:5: "The plans of the diligent lead surely to abundance, but every one who is hasty comes only to want."

Luke 14:28–30: "For which of you, desiring to build a tower, does not first sit down and count the cost, whether he has enough to complete it? Otherwise, when he has laid a foundation, and is not able to finish, all who see it begin to mock him, saying, 'This man began to build, and was not able to finish.'"

Catechism 2342: "Self-mastery is a long and exacting work. One can never consider it acquired once and for all. It presupposes renewed effort at all stages of life."

## Reading

Is planning important? It may not seem fun, but think of the effort a football team puts into preparing for its games. They work out to make sure they're in top physical condition. They watch films of opponents to learn what to expect. They develop a game plan that utilizes their strengths. They practice plays over and over until they know them in their sleep. They have a plan and they work that plan in order to achieve their objective—in this case, winning a football game.

## The Importance of Planning

To succeed at anything takes a combination of foresight, desire, strategy, and solid execution. That's true in sports, school, career, and just about everything important in life. It's also true in your financial life. In short, succeeding in life requires a game plan and the discipline to live it out.

It's odd. We plan for things every day, big and small. We plan for school exams. We plan parties. We even plan what clothes we'll wear each day. But when it comes to making financial plans, many people choose just to wing it. There's a saying that "When you fail to plan, you are planning to fail." If a football team isn't well prepared, they lose their game. If a violinist doesn't practice, he may sound like chalk screeching across a chalkboard.

Failing to manage your finances properly will hurt you. You'll find your money controlling you rather than the other way around. When that happens, you become money's slave. Lack of planning leads to chaos. In marriage, a lack of financial planning leads to tension and arguments that can in turn lead to divorce. Planning as a steward of Providence will help you reach your financial and life goals for the future.

God is okay with the process of planning, as long as we always place our plans at his feet. In Tobit 4:19, we are encouraged to pray about our plans: "Bless the Lord God on every occasion; ask him that your ways may be made straight and that all your paths and plans may prosper."

Good planning means taking care of the resources we have: "Know well the condition of your flocks, and give attention to your herds." (Proverbs 27:23) In Biblical times, people often made their living through agriculture. Livestock was crucial to their survival. You may not be caring, literally, for herds like the ones referred to in Proverbs, but these words of guidance are as applicable to the care of your home, cars, tools, and work-related equipment as the herds were to the old-timers of the Bible.

It can be tempting to take shortcuts, but God warns of consequences when we do so: "The plans of the diligent lead surely to abundance, but every one who is hasty comes only to want." (Proverbs 21:5) In the Gospel of Luke 14:28–30, he gives a very specific example that all builders can relate to: "For which of you, desiring to build a tower, does not first sit down and count the cost, whether he has enough to complete it? Otherwise, when he has laid a foundation, and is not able to finish, all who see it begin to mock him, saying, 'This man began to build, and was not able to finish.'"

Clearly, planning is an important part of success. What does that mean when it comes to your money? What is a financial plan?

Think of it as a road map that helps you get from where you are today to where you want to be in the future, whether that's next month, next year, or forty years from now. It's a guide for developing and using the resources God has entrusted to you to meet the growing responsibilities you will have in future years. It includes understanding how you will generate income, prioritize expenses, grow assets, and manage debts.

Developing a financial plan isn't rocket science, but there are a few terms and tools that are important for you to learn. These are just the building blocks you'll need to manage your money well. They aren't an end in themselves. But they are a critical part of the financial planning process.

Financial planning is a marathon, not a sprint. The Catechism tells us that "Self-mastery is a long and exacting work. One can never consider it acquired once and for all. It presupposes renewed effort at all stages of life" (CCC 2342). Does a pro football player ever get tired of all the physical training and practice sessions? He wouldn't be human if he didn't. But those are the means to his goal of winning games. It's the same with the basics of financial planning. There will be times when you wish your money issues would take care of themselves, just like your wishes about homework and the dishes and every other tedious task. Persevere. The rewards of managing your money as a steward of Providence are abundant and worth the effort, so let's get started!

# Examples of Assets

| |
|---|
| Checking account |
| Mutual funds |
| Boat |
| Money Market fund |
| Bonds |
| Jewelry |
| Certificates of deposit |
| Real estate |
| Antiques |
| Stocks |
| Automobiles |
| Cash surrender value of life insurance |

The following Stewart family balance sheet reflects a realistic example of what one might look like for a family with three young children. It has some weak points that you will discuss later in this session's class activity.

The makeup of your balance sheet should change dramatically over the years, with a growing base of assets to help pay for future responsibilities, and a declining debt balance as college loans and mortgages are paid off.

## The Balance Sheet

A balance sheet is a snapshot of your financial position at one point in time. It is a summary of assets and liabilities. An asset is something of value that you own. A liability represents a debt that you owe. Net worth equals assets minus liabilities.

# Examples of Liabilities

| |
|---|
| Mortgage |
| Home equity loan |
| Auto loan |
| Student loan |
| Business loan |
| Credit card debt |

# Stewart Family Balance Sheet

| Description | Current Year | Prior Year |
|---|---|---|
| **Assets** | | |
| | | |
| **Cash and Cash Equivalents** | | |
| Cash on Hand | 100 | 100 |
| Cash - Checking | 1,100 | 1,100 |
| Cash - Money Market | - | - |
| Cash - Other | - | - |
| Total Cash and Cash Equivalents | 1,200 | 1,200 |
| | | |
| **Invested Assets** | | |
| Certificates of Deposit | - | - |
| Brokerage Accounts | - | - |
| Retirement Plans | 12,000 | 11,000 |
| Business Investment | - | - |
| Total Invested Assets | 12,000 | 11,000 |
| | | |
| **Use Assets** | | |
| House | 250,000 | 240,000 |
| Autos | 15,000 | 17,000 |
| Other | 10,000 | 10,000 |
| Total Use Assets | 275,000 | 267,000 |
| | | |
| **Total Assets** | 288,200 | 279,200 |
| | | |
| **Liabilities** | | |
| Mortgage and Home Equity Loans | 200,000 | 203,000 |
| Auto Loans | 10,000 | 12,000 |
| Credit Cards and Installment Loans | 10,000 | 7,000 |
| Student Loans | - | - |
| Business Debt | - | - |
| Other (Loans from Family and Friends; Retirement Plans; Life Insurance) | - | - |
| | | |
| **Total Liabilities** | 220,000 | 222,000 |
| | | |
| **Net Worth** | 68,200 | 57,200 |

## The Budget

While the balance sheet focuses on assets and liabilities and is a picture of your finances at one point in time, a budget is a summary of income and expenses over a chosen period of time.

My personal preference is to use annual budgets. Why? I want a time frame that's long enough to see the big picture—one that makes it possible to capture all the expenses I expect to incur during the course of a year. Some people like to break budgets into monthly or even weekly amounts. But it's a lot of work to break non-recurring expenses into monthly amounts. I find the annual approach works just fine.

On the following page is an example of what the Stewart family's annual budget looks like. Notice the many types of income and expenses included in a basic family budget. You'll also note that there are several problems with their budget. For example, spending exceeds income, and actual spending for several categories doesn't match planned spending in those categories. Their priorities are a bit out of sync. Your class activity will include balancing this family's budget.

# Stewart Family Budget Review

| Account Description | Estimated Annual Income/Expenses | Actual Annual % | Guideline Budget | Guideline Budget % |
|---|---|---|---|---|
| **Gross Income** | 80,000 | 100% | 80,000 | 100% |
| Salary | 75,000 | | | |
| Bonus | 2,000 | | | |
| Interest | - | | | |
| Dividends | - | | | |
| Retirement Plan | - | | | |
| Other | 3,000 | | | |
| | | | | |
| **Tithe/Giving** | 800 | 1% | 8,000 | 10% |
| Deductible | 800 | | | |
| Non-deductible | - | | | |
| Children Tuition | - | | | |
| | | | | |
| **Taxes** | 13,600 | 17% | 12,000 | 15% |
| Federal Income | 5,000 | | | |
| State Income | 2,000 | | | |
| Social Security | 5,000 | | | |
| Medicare | 1,200 | | | |
| State Disability | 400 | | | |
| | | | | |
| **Current Education** | 200 | 0% | 800 | 1% |
| Tuition (See tithe) | - | | | |
| Supplies | 200 | | | |
| Day Care | - | | | |
| Other | - | | | |
| | | | | |
| **Savings** | - | 0% | 7,200 | 9% |
| Emergency and Rainy Day | - | | | |
| Future Education | - | | | |
| Retirement Plan | - | | | |
| | | | | |
| **Housing and Home Expenses** | 30,400 | 38% | 24,800 | 31% |
| Mortgage/rent | 18,000 | | | |
| Insurance | 800 | | | |
| Taxes | 3,000 | | | |
| Electricity | 1,000 | | | |
| Gas | 900 | | | |
| Water | 800 | | | |
| Gardening | 800 | | | |
| Housecleaning | - | | | |
| Telephone | 1,000 | | | |
| Maintenance | 1,500 | | | |
| Pest Control | 400 | | | |
| Association Dues | - | | | |
| Bottled Water | - | | | |
| Postage | 200 | | | |
| Miscellaneous | - | | | |
| Improvements | 2,000 | | | |
| | | | | |
| **Groceries** | 11,200 | 14% | 8,800 | 11% |
| | | | | |
| **Transportation** | 7,700 | 10% | 8,000 | 10% |

| Account Description | Estimated Annual Income/Expenses | Actual Annual % | Guideline Budget | Guideline Budget % |
|---|---|---|---|---|
| Payment/Replacement Savings | 3,600 | | | |
| Gas/Oil | 2,000 | | | |
| Insurance | 800 | | | |
| License/Taxes | 300 | | | |
| Maintenance/Repair | 1,000 | | | |
| **Medical Expenses** | 2,400 | 3% | 2,400 | 3% |
| Doctor | 1,500 | | | |
| Dentist | 500 | | | |
| Prescriptions | 400 | | | |
| Other | - | | | |
| **Insurance** | 2,400 | 3% | 2,400 | 3% |
| Medical | 900 | | | |
| Life | 1,500 | | | |
| Disability | - | | | |
| **Debt Payments** | 3,500 | 4% | - | 0% |
| Credit Card | 3,500 | | | |
| Loans and Notes | - | | | |
| Other | - | | | |
| **Clothing** | 4,000 | 5% | 1,600 | 2% |
| **Entertain. and Recreation** | 5,100 | 6% | 2,400 | 3% |
| Eating Out | 3,300 | | | |
| Babysitting | - | | | |
| Cable/Satellite/Movies | 800 | | | |
| Allowances | - | | | |
| Activities | - | | | |
| Vacation | 1,000 | | | |
| **Work Related** | - | 0% | - | 0% |
| Education/Dues | - | | | |
| Internet/Phone | - | | | |
| Other | - | | | |
| **Miscellaneous** | 3,200 | 4% | 1,600 | 2% |
| Beauty/Barber/Cosmetics | 800 | | | |
| Laundry | 200 | | | |
| Subscriptions | 200 | | | |
| Holiday/Gifts | 1,700 | | | |
| Accounting/Legal | 100 | | | |
| Veterinarian/Animals | 200 | | | |
| **Summary of Inc./Exp.** | | | | |
| Total Income | 80,000 | 100% | 80,000 | 100% |
| Total Expenses | 84,500 | 106% | 80,000 | 100% |
| Income Over/(Under) Exp. | (4,500) | -6% | - | 0% |

Because a balance sheet is a listing of assets and liabilities at one point in time, it's easier to compile than a budget. You just need to have access to the latest statements from your banks, brokerage houses, and lenders. A budget is a bit more complicated since it captures income and spending patterns over a period of time. It normally takes a few months before you develop confidence that your budget is a true reflection of what's really going on.

## Managing Non-Recurring Income and Expenses

Income and expenses sometimes occur at regular intervals. Examples include weekly or biweekly paychecks or monthly rent and utility bills. But not all financial activity occurs on such a regular basis. Examples of non-recurring activity include bonuses, property taxes, license fees, insurance, repairs and maintenance, among others. Non-recurring expenses are one of the reasons I use an annual budget, since it makes it much easier to factor in these types of expenses. Make sure you consider the types of non-recurring income and expenses that impact you and make them a part of your budget.

## Cash and the Envelope System

One very simple way to budget is the envelope system. It's been in use since long before computers ever existed! I don't suggest that it be your primary budgeting tool, but it can help you manage the cash you spend much more effectively. Here's how it works:

Think through those budget categories that you regularly use cash for—especially those areas where you have a difficult time controlling spending. These may include groceries, eating out, or other forms of entertainment and recreation. Create a separate envelope for each category. Each pay period, place your budgeted amount of cash for that category into the envelope. Once the envelope's empty, you know you can't spend any more on that category until the next pay period. It's a surefire way to help you stick to your spending plan in these areas.

## Tracking Income and Expenses: A Key Step

Tracking income and expenses is important both before you establish a budget and after. Do you know where your money is going? You probably have some vague sense, but until you actually track your daily spending by category, it's hard to know where it all went—especially all those ATM withdrawals! Tracking your income and spending for thirty days is a great exercise to do before you create your first budget. It will give you confidence that the budget you set up is realistic.

Once you've prepared your budget, you need to continue to track your actual income and expenses by category. Thankfully, computers have made doing this easier than it used to be. Preparing a budget isn't a one-time thing that you can just forget about. Like a business, you need to compare periodically what is really happening to what you said would happen. That's the only way you'll know if your plan is working—and that's where many people falter. They never compare their actual income and expenses to their original plan. Don't let this happen to you.

## Checkbook Management

Since your checkbook register is your initial place to record most of your financial transactions, it's important to keep it up-to-date. You want to make sure you have a good record of all of your purchases, and even more important, you want to know how much money you have in the bank.

Have you ever heard someone say, "I must have money since I still have checks?" It might be nice if the bank looked at it that way, but—surprise, surprise—they don't. In fact, they'll charge some hefty fees if you write bad checks, also known as NSF or Not Sufficient Fund checks.

# Financial Toolbox

**Visit www.VeritasFinancialMinistries.com and register to use *My Veritas Plan*. It's free!**

You can prepare your *balance sheet* and *budget*, track your *income* and *expenses*, and use lots of useful *calculators*!

The bank will offer to set up what they call overdraft protection, which means that they'll process your check even though you don't have enough money in the account. It's a fancy name for borrowing money, because they do make you pay it back, and they'll charge you a pretty penny on the amount you borrowed. Don't use overdraft protection. Manage your checkbook like a pro.

The first and most important step in maintaining your checkbook register is to make sure to enter all checking account transactions. Of course this includes all checks written, but it also means deposits, withdrawals (including ATM), online bill pay, bank charges, and interest earned. If you take after your parents' generation, you'll use a manual check register (paper and pen); the more technologically inclined have a broad range of software options for maintaining their register. The concepts we're discussing apply to both, it's just that the software programs do more (but not all!) of the work for you.

## Carbon Copy Checks

Even young people who are technologically savvy need to write a paper check once in a while. For these situations, there's a great tool you can't do without—carbon copy checks. Have you ever written a check for

# Sample Check Register

| Number or Code | Date | Transaction Description | Payment | Deposit | Balance |
|---|---|---|---|---|---|
| Bill Pay | 2/5 | Insurance Co. | 108.17 | | 522.33 |
| 102 | 2/6 | Auto Co. | 235.00 | | 287.33 |
| 103 | 2/8 | Sharon's Supermarket | 58.05 | | 229.28 |
| ATM | 2/9 | Cash withdrawal | 50.00 | | 179.28 |
| Auto Deposit | 2/10 | Deposit from work | | 100.00 | 279.28 |
| Service Charge | 2/12 | Bank service charge | 2.50 | | 276.78 |

something, and in the hurry of the moment forgotten to record it in the check register? It's easy to do and it's frustrating—you feel like pulling your hair out when you realize your mistake and try to retrace your steps. Carbon copy checks eliminate that problem by providing an automatic record of every check you write. They cost a bit more, but will save you in the end.

## Online Bill Pay and Checkbook Management

Online bill pay is one of the marvelous contributions of new technology to personal finance. It makes it easy to pay many of your vendors, and saves you time and postage. But it doesn't eliminate the need for you to control and manage your checking account. Based on my experience,

people now use multiple payment channels, including:

- Auto pay features at vendor sites, using a debit or credit card

- Bill pay feature provided by their bank

- Financial planning software that includes bill payment features

- Cash

- Paper checks

- Debit and credit cards at point of purchase

Because multiple payment channels continue to be used, and more importantly, because banks do make mistakes, online bill pay has not eliminated the need for an appropriate set of checks and balances. No pun intended! You need a way to track your checking account activity that is independent of your bank's record of transactions. And you need to "reconcile" your activity to the activity of the bank periodically. You can do this on a monthly basis using the bank statement provided by the bank, or more frequently by checking your activity online. For detailed instructions on how to do a bank reconciliation, see the Appendix.

## Making Bank Deposits and Withdrawals

When you make a deposit at the bank, you'll be expected to complete a deposit ticket. This is a summary of your deposit information, including how much cash and a list of check amounts with a grand total for the amount of the deposit.

If you want to withdraw cash from your account, you'll need to fill out a withdrawal ticket. Most bank forms include a section for your account number, the amount you want to withdraw, the date, and your signature. Banks will want to verify your identity, so make sure you have your driver's license or other photo identification available.

Remember to update your checkbook register once you have completed your transaction.

## Summary

My brother-in-law is a priest. He once shared a Latin saying with me: "Serva ordinem, et ordo servabit te," which means, "Serve order and order will serve you." Those words contain a lot of truth! By developing and continuing to "work" your financial plan, not only will you always know where you are financially, but you'll be able to anticipate where you need to be in the future, along with the steps you should be taking today to get there. Great freedom comes with that knowledge.

## Discussion Topics

Read the discussion topic questions and write down your thoughts. This should be done prior to your class or small group get-together. In your class or small group, you'll share your thoughts with each other. For those discussion topics that list a Bible or Catechism reference, review it by referring to the applicable text at the beginning of the session.

# Discussion Topic 1
# Proverbs 21:5

It's important to make financial plans, but it is also important to be flexible when your situation changes. How can you strike the balance between being a good financial planner and an overly attached controller?

_____

_____

_____

_____

_____

_____

_____

_____

_____

_____

## Discussion Topic 2
## Catechism 2342

List five reasons for living on a budget. List five consequences of not living on a budget. What gets in the way of people living on a budget?

_____

_____

_____

_____

_____

_____

_____

_____

_____

_____

## Activity

Follow the instructions of your teacher/leader as he (or she) guides you through this session's activity. The activity is designed to help you apply the concepts learned in this session in a fun and engaging way.

Session Five

# Wealth: How to Create It, How to Use It

## Session Objectives

**◌** Understand the purpose of wealth.

**◌** Explain compound earnings.

**◌** Create awareness of the need for emergency, rainy day, and reserve saving funds.

**◌** Understand diversification, asset allocation, the types of assets that fit within a typical asset allocation model, and what it means to rebalance an investment portfolio.

**◌** Recognize the relationship between risk and return. Explain the Rule of 72.

**◌** Understand how debt magnifies gains and losses when used in investing.

𝓬 Explain how tax-favored investments play a part in meeting financial goals.

𝓬 Understand the risks of trying to get rich quick.

## Key Terms

| | | |
|---|---|---|
| Detachment | Compound Earnings | Interest |
| Capital Gain | Rate of Return | Rule of 72 |
| Risk/Return Relationship | Money Market Fund | Certificate of Deposit |
| Diversification | Asset Allocation | Stock |
| Bond | Commodities | Mutual Fund |
| Rebalancing | Tax-Free and Tax-Favored Investments | |

Reserve Funds: Emergency, Rainy Day, Retirement, College

## Bible and Catechism References

Catechism 2404: "The ownership of any property makes its holder a steward of Providence, *with the task of making it fruitful* [emphasis mine] and communicating its benefits to others, first of all his family."

Matthew 25:20–21: "'Master, you delivered to me five talents; here I have made five talents more.' His master said to him, 'Well done, good and faithful servant; you have been faithful over a little, I will set you over much; enter into the joy of your Master.'"

Matthew 25:24-30: "He also who had received the one talent came forward, saying, 'Master, I knew you to be a hard man, reaping where you did not sow, and gathering where you did not winnow; so I was afraid, and I went and hid your talent in the ground. Here you have what is yours.' But his master answered him, 'You wicked and slothful servant! You knew that I reap where I have not sowed, and gather where I have not winnowed? Then you ought to have invested my money with the bankers, and at my coming I should have received what was my own with interest. So take the talent from him, and give it to him who has the ten talents. For to everyone who has will more be given, and he will have abundance; but from him who has not, even what he has will be taken away. And cast the worthless servant into the outer darkness, where there will be weeping and gnashing of teeth.'"

Matthew 6:24: "No one can serve two masters; for either he will hate the one and love the other, or he will be devoted to the one and despise the other. You cannot serve God and mammon."

Mark 8:36: "For what does it profit for a man, to gain the whole world and forfeit his life?"

Luke 12:16-21: "And he told them a parable, saying, 'The land of a rich man brought forth plentifully; and he thought to himself, "What shall I do, for I have nowhere to store my crops?" And he said, "I will do this: I will pull down my barns, and build larger ones; and there I will store all my grain and my goods. And I will say to my soul, Soul, you have ample goods laid up for many years; take your ease, eat, drink, be merry." But God said to him, "Fool! This night your soul is required of you; and the things you have prepared, whose will they be?" So is he who lays up treasure for himself, and is not rich toward God.'"

Genesis 41:34-36: "Let Pharaoh proceed to appoint overseers over the land, and take the fifth part of the produce of the land of Egypt during the seven plenteous years. And let them gather all the food of these good years that are coming, and lay up grain under the authority of Pharaoh for food in the cities, and let them keep it. That food shall be a reserve for the land against the seven years of famine which are to befall the land of Egypt, so that the land may not perish through the famine."

Proverbs 21:20: "Precious treasure remains in a wise man's dwelling, but a foolish man devours it."

Ecclesiastes 11:2: "Give a portion to seven, or even to eight, for you know not what evil may happen on earth."

Proverbs 13:11: "Wealth hastily gotten will dwindle, but he who gathers little by little will increase it."

Proverbs 28:20: "A faithful man will abound with blessings, but he who hastens to be rich will not go unpunished."

## Reading

Without a doubt some of you are thinking the topic of creating and using wealth will only apply to you in the distant future. . . . Think again! I admit that some of the concepts in this session are a bit technical and will impact you to a greater degree once you get your career and family life underway. But let me stress the fact that they are important concepts for you to understand now.

The concepts about wealth creation are important, but even more important is the impact of the life choices you make today on your ability to create wealth in the future. Emphasizing your education, learning good work habits, keeping out of debt, avoiding addictive behaviors, and reserving your sexuality (and its responsibilities) for marriage are all ways that provide a solid foundation for launching your years of creating wealth. Mistakes in these areas today may negatively impact your ability to reach your financial goals far into the future.

## Wealth: A Responsibility to Create It, A Responsibility to Use It for Good Purposes

Notice anything striking about this session's references from the Bible? They seem to contradict each other. On the one hand, you hear praise for saving and increasing wealth. On the other hand, there are some pretty harsh warnings related to wealth. So which is it?

A steward of Providence has the responsibility to create wealth. As the Catechism says, "The ownership of any property makes its holder a steward of Providence, with the task of making it fruitful." (CCC 2404)

The parable of the talents (Matthew 25:20–30) is primarily about growing our faith, but the example Jesus uses makes it clear that he expects us to grow our resources, too. The steward who provided a good return is praised, while the steward that buried his gifts is chastised.

Even Pope Benedict has, when discussing the subject of poverty, spoken of the need to create wealth. He said that trying to solve the problem of poverty solely by redistribution of existing wealth is an "illusion," and that "wealth creation therefore becomes an inescapable duty, which must be kept in mind if the fight against material poverty is to be effective in the long run."

Wealth creation is a responsibility. The challenge—and hence the Lord's warnings (Matt. 6:24; Mark 8:36; Luke 12:16–21)—is to respond to wealth in ways that honor God and neighbor. How do we do that?

- Give the Lord first place in your life. Follow his teaching for life and you'll be confident in your priorities. Remember that money is just an object that can't compete with the Creator.

- Know that you won't leave this world with any possessions, but that you will give an accounting to the Lord for how you used the possessions he entrusted to you during your life on earth.

○ If blessed with wealth beyond the needs of you and your family, have the good judgment to use that wealth wisely. Remember that the saints frequently point to simplicity and detachment from things, lest the Lord be crowded out.

○ Avoid attitudes of selfishness and laziness described in the parable of the rich farmer (Luke 12:16–21). Not only was he keeping everything for himself, but since he had it made, he planned on kicking back and relaxing—forgetting that the talents he had were to be used for good purposes. We never stop being a steward of Providence.

It's an interesting paradox. Stewards of Providence are called to create wealth, yet Jesus' admonitions about attachments to money remain as true as ever. The challenge is this: To use our talents to create wealth, yet remain detached from that wealth and use it for good purposes. Keeping that balance is a challenge, but a mature Christian is up to the task.

"May you consider truly good whatever leads to your goal and truly evil whatever makes you fall away from it. Prosperity and adversity, wealth and poverty, health and sickness, honors and humiliations, life and death, in the mind of the wise man, are not to be sought for their own sake, nor avoided for their own sake. But if they contribute to the glory of God and your eternal happiness, then they are good and should be sought. If they detract from this, they are evil and must be avoided."
—**St. Robert Bellarmine**

## Wealth Creation: The Multiplier Effect

There are many paths to creating wealth, but, other than inheriting it, they all have one thing in common: a multiplier effect.

In business, the multiplier effect comes from an expanding base of customers that needs or wants the product or service you offer. As long as the growth is managed well, increasing revenues lead to profits that allow you to continue to grow, do a great deal of good by employing greater numbers of people, provide a good financial return to you and other shareholders, and be generous in your community.

Of course, coming up with the idea and managing the start-up and growth of a business is no piece of cake. But remember that even some corporate giants started small and grew from there. Consider these:

⊙ Walmart

⊙ Starbucks

⊙ Chick-fil-A

No doubt, some of you have an entrepreneurial spirit. By applying the principles learned in this program and some additional education and mentoring, you can grow a business, create wealth, and make a real and positive difference in your surroundings.

## The Miracle of Compound Earnings

While many people make their living running a business, the vast majority work as employees for someone else. How does one create wealth when compensation is in the form of salary rather than ownership of a company?

Salary levels certainly play a part in determining the level of wealth one can create; but just as important is being a disciplined saver and investor. There are many stories of people who made a lot of money during their life but ended up broke. There are also many examples of folks who worked hard for years and years and created wealth you never would have thought possible given their salary. How did they do it? Not by running to the poker tables on payday. They did it by consistently saving and investing a portion of their salary over a long period of time.

In this case, the multiplier effect is compound earnings. Einstein called this remarkable little concept the greatest mathematical discovery of all time. How it works: Compound earnings accrue when invested money grows as a result of interest or capital gains on the original investment. As money continues to be invested and continues to earn a positive return, it multiplies over time in a very significant way.

Here's an example. Starting at age 25, Matt and Maria save $5,000 every year until they are 65. Their investments grow at 8% until they retire. At that point, Matt and Maria's investments have grown to $1,194,706.

What happens if you wait to start investing? When it comes to the power of compound earnings, time really *is* money! Let's look at

# The Power of Compounding Interest

| Age | Matt and Maria Savings | Matt and Maria Savings and Compound Interest | Greg and Laura Savings | Greg and Laura Savings and Compound Interest |
|---|---|---|---|---|
| 26 | 5,000 | 5,000 | 0 | 0 |
| 27 | 5,000 | 10,400 | 0 | 0 |
| 28 | 5,000 | 16,232 | 0 | 0 |
| 29 | 5,000 | 22,531 | 0 | 0 |
| 30 | 5,000 | 29,333 | 0 | 0 |
| 31 | 5,000 | 36,680 | 0 | 0 |
| 32 | 5,000 | 44,614 | 0 | 0 |
| 33 | 5,000 | 53,183 | 0 | 0 |
| 34 | 5,000 | 62,438 | 0 | 0 |
| 35 | 5,000 | 72,433 | 0 | 0 |
| 36 | 5,000 | 83,227 | 5,000 | 5,000 |
| 37 | 5,000 | 94,886 | 5,000 | 10,400 |
| 38 | 5,000 | 107,476 | 5,000 | 16,232 |
| 39 | 5,000 | 121,075 | 5,000 | 22,531 |
| 40 | 5,000 | 135,761 | 5,000 | 29,333 |
| 41 | 5,000 | 151,621 | 5,000 | 36,680 |
| 42 | 5,000 | 168,751 | 5,000 | 44,614 |
| 43 | 5,000 | 187,251 | 5,000 | 53,183 |
| 44 | 5,000 | 207,231 | 5,000 | 62,438 |
| 45 | 5,000 | 228,810 | 5,000 | 72,433 |
| 46 | 5,000 | 252,115 | 5,000 | 83,227 |
| 47 | 5,000 | 277,284 | 5,000 | 94,886 |
| 48 | 5,000 | 304,466 | 5,000 | 107,476 |
| 49 | 5,000 | 333,824 | 5,000 | 121,075 |
| 50 | 5,000 | 365,530 | 5,000 | 135,761 |
| 51 | 5,000 | 399,772 | 5,000 | 151,621 |
| 52 | 5,000 | 436,754 | 5,000 | 168,751 |
| 53 | 5,000 | 476,694 | 5,000 | 187,251 |
| 54 | 5,000 | 519,830 | 5,000 | 207,231 |
| 55 | 5,000 | 566,416 | 5,000 | 228,810 |
| 56 | 5,000 | 616,729 | 5,000 | 252,115 |
| 57 | 5,000 | 671,068 | 5,000 | 277,284 |
| 58 | 5,000 | 729,753 | 5,000 | 304,466 |
| 59 | 5,000 | 793,133 | 5,000 | 333,824 |
| 60 | 5,000 | 861,584 | 5,000 | 365,530 |
| 61 | 5,000 | 935,511 | 5,000 | 399,772 |
| 62 | 5,000 | 1,015,352 | 5,000 | 436,754 |
| 63 | 5,000 | 1,101,580 | 5,000 | 476,694 |
| 64 | 5,000 | 1,194,706 | 5,000 | 519,830 |
| **Total** | **195,000** | **1,194,706** | **145,000** | **519,830** |

another example. Greg and Laura don't start saving until they're 35. Just like Matt and Maria, they contribute $5,000 a year until they turn 65, but they started ten years later. Their investments also grow at 8% each year. But they end up with only $519,830. See why it's so important to start saving early?

The table on the previous page shows how these examples work year by year.

You can see the power of compound earnings—especially in the later years. Because Matt and Maria started saving and investing early and were consistent, they not only have twice the retirement balance that Greg and Laura do, but the amount they will earn each year on that balance will also be twice as high.

# The Rule of 72

A simple rule that can help you understand how the rate of return impacts the growth of an investment is the Rule of 72. It provides a simple way to know how long it will take for your investment to double. The calculation is simple:

**72 ÷ Interest Rate\* = Doubling Time in Years**

For example:

72 ÷ 3 = 24 Years

72 ÷ 8 = 9 Years

72 ÷ 10 = 7.2 Years

72 ÷ 12 = 6 Years

\*Interest rate is assumed to be an annually compounded rate.

Notice that the growth of the investments in the table is only partly owing to the amount saved. The majority of the growth came from the rate of return that compounded their investment over time.

Let's return to the examples of Matt and Maria and Greg and Laura. If they had invested the same amount but been able to achieve a 10% rate of return rather than 8%, the difference in their retirement balances would have been even greater. Matt and Maria would have had $2,007,239 when they turned 65, while Greg and Laura would have had only $743,155.

## The Relationship between Risk and Rate of Return

If it were easy to earn a high rate of return, investing would be easy, and everyone would succeed. But that's not the way it is. History shows that there is a relationship between risk and rate of return. Achieving a higher rate of return requires accepting higher levels of risk as well.

One may achieve a low rate of return (say 2–3%) with very low risk (think Certificate of Deposit or Treasury bill). But in most cases that level of return won't grow your investments at the rate necessary to meet future needs, such as college education and retirement.

Speculators may find an investment (think Las Vegas) that could double their money (100% return), but there is also a reasonably high probability that they will lose their complete investment as well (-100% return).

How do you balance the relationship between risk and return? It comes back to having a financial plan—knowing where you are today, and where you want to be tomorrow or thirty years from now. Someone just getting out of college and starting a career is in a position to be a more aggressive investor, while most retirees will need to be more cautious. Once you understand where you are today, where you want to go, and your time frame for getting there, you can choose the types of investments that make the most sense for you.

Be aware and take advantage of tax-free and tax-favored investment opportunities. In an effort to encourage certain types of behavior (saving for retirement and college, and investing in the infrastructure of the country), the government provides a number of investment opportunities that come with certain tax benefits. Such things as 401K retirement plans, 529 college saving plans, and state and municipal bonds can increase after-tax rates of return on your overall investment portfolio.

## Building a Savings and Investment Model for the Future: First Things First

A big, bad, and highly common mistake people make is failing to save and invest for future obligations. Then when they find themselves in a financial hole, they dig a bigger one by borrowing.

You can avoid this trap. After you've given a portion of your increase back to the Lord in the form of charitable giving (first fruits), set aside the savings you'll need for the future. Then you can use your remaining income for regular living expenses.
If you don't make savings a part of your plan, you won't save.

Once you get out of school and start your career and family life, what should your savings strategy consist of? It makes sense to take care of some basics first. Make sure you have an initial emergency fund of about $5,000. Then pay down any unproductive debt you have, especially high-interest-rate credit card debt. Next, develop a rainy day fund. It should consist of at least six months' expenses, but a year would be better.

Once you have your rainy day fund, you'll want to save for your retirement needs, and the cost of college for your children, to the extent you plan on assisting them. When it comes to funding these, you'll use separate investment accounts since you'll most likely be taking advantage of tax-favored investments. The power of the Internet makes planning for these events a whole lot easier. There are many calculators available to help you determine how much you need to save today in order to meet your future financial goals.

Finally, you'll want to set up a reserve fund for other long-term purchases (beyond a year). Examples include funds for replacing a vehicle, repaying college debt, making a down payment or improvements on a home, taking a dream vacation, or assisting with the cost of a child's wedding. I suggest keeping these reserve funds in one money market fund or shorter-term certificate of deposit, since they will normally be needed within five years, which is too short a time frame for more volatile investments. You can keep track of the various portions of the fund by using a simple spreadsheet. Here is an example of how you can use a reserve fund to pay cash for a car rather than borrow unproductively:

# How to Use a Reserve Fund to Pay Cash for Your Next Car

| | |
|---|---|
| **Anticipated timing of purchase** | 3 years from now |
| **Estimated purchase price of car** | $15,000 |
| **Annual savings required** | $5,000 |
| **Paycheck frequency** | Every two weeks |
| **Amount to be direct-deposited into automobile reserve fund every pay period** | $192.30 |

By following this simple approach, you'll have the $15,000 you need when it's time to buy your next car. Best of all, you'll be debt free!

Here is a summary of how you should set savings and investment priorities:

## Savings and Investment Sequence

| | |
|---|---|
| **Priority 1** | Emergency Fund—$5,000 |
| **Priority 2** | Eliminate Unproductive Debt |
| **Priority 3** | Rainy Day Fund: 6–12 Months Expenses |
| **Priority 4** | Retirement Fund |
| **Priority 5** | Reserve Fund: College, House Down Payment or Improvements, Auto Replacement, Weddings |

## Diversification and Asset Allocation

There's an old saying that you shouldn't "put all your eggs in one basket." That same concept applies to your investments. The principle is even scriptural. Ecclesiastes 11:2 says, "Give a portion to seven, or even to eight, for you know not what evil may happen on earth."

You want to spread your investments over a number of asset types. For example, you don't want your retirement plan to consist solely of shares in your employer's stock. Too many people approaching retirement have watched their nest egg disappear before their eyes when employers go bankrupt.

Asset allocation is one strategy that helps investors develop a diversified investment portfolio that balances the risk/return relationship. In today's confusing investment world, you can own stocks, bonds, commodities, and almost any other type of asset class you can think of. You can invest in small companies or large companies, domestic or international. You can own individual stocks or bonds, or you can own baskets of assets through mutual funds or several other types of investment funds.

Younger people with a long investing horizon often allocate their investments more heavily toward higher growth—but also higher risk—asset classes, like small company stocks. As one nears retirement, it becomes important to reduce financial risk, so one's portfolio allocation may shift more toward fixed income investments like bonds.

## Rebalancing a Portfolio: Taking the Emotion Out of Investing Decisions

The great investor, Warren Buffett, frequently says, "Be greedy when others are fearful and fearful when others are greedy." His point is that investors often make decisions based on emotion and on how others are acting. When the market is at a peak and everyone is feeling good it is probably a time to look ahead for the painful correction that may be due. Conversely, when the market is performing poorly and everyone's emotions are frayed it is often a time of great opportunity.

A simple way to take the emotion out of investing decisions is to do what is known as rebalancing your portfolio. Because markets tend to do their thing (rise and fall) without asking the investor what he'd prefer, what you've allocated to specific asset classes might need periodic adjusting to keep in line with your financial goals. Different asset classes, for example, behave in different ways at different times. The stock market may be soaring while bonds are taking a dive. Rebalancing simply means that as your asset allocation strays from your original plan as a result of the different rates of return of various asset classes, you periodically (quarterly, semi-annually, or annually) sell the asset classes that have overperformed and reinvest the proceeds in the classes that have underperformed. Here is an example in chart form of how it works:

# Rebalancing Your Portfolio

| Asset Class | Original Allocation | Current Allocation Owing to Market Performance | Allocation after Rebalancing |
|---|---|---|---|
| Small company stocks | 50,000 (20%) | 60,000 (22%) | 55,250 (20%) |
| Large company stocks | 50,000 (20%) | 55,000 (20%) | 55,250 (20%) |
| Bonds | 50,000 (20%) | 52,000 (19%) | 55,250 (20%) |
| International stocks | 50,000 (20%) | 65,000 (23%) | 55,250 (20%) |
| Commodities | 25,000 (10%) | 20,000 (7%) | 28,000 (10%) |
| Cash | 25,000 (10%) | 25,000 (9%) | 28,000 (10%) |
| Total | 250,000 (100%) | 277,000 (100%) | 277,000 (100%) |

Rebalancing provides a systematic way to buy low and sell high. As you get more involved with investing, seek counsel from people you trust. Certified financial planners are a good place to start. They can help you develop your goals and a plan that will help you reach them.

## Debt and Wealth Creation, Debt and Wealth Destruction

We'll be covering basics of debt management in the next session, including the cautious attitude that Scripture advises. But that caution doesn't mean that debt can't be used in productive ways—as long as there are proper "rules of the road" and adequate "guardrails." Borrowing prudently to purchase appreciating assets is a productive use of debt. Home ownership is a good example of this.

Another example would be to use debt to pay for the expansion of a business when the rate of return is expected to exceed the cost of borrowing. The trick is to know your business well enough to understand the level and type of debt that makes sense. When used appropriately, such debt has a positive multiplier effect. When a business is overleveraged (too much debt), the business often fails and the owner's investment may be completely wiped out.

# Productive Use of Debt

Here is an example of how an appropriate use of debt creates a positive multiplier effect:

| | |
|---|---|
| **Original investment:** | $50,000 |
| **Add debt used:** | $50,000 (50% leverage ratio) |
| **Total investment:** | $100,000 |
| **Asset value 10 years later:** | $220,000 |
| **10-year rate of return without debt:** | 120%: ($220,000-$100,000)/$100,000 |
| **10-year rate of return with debt:** | 240%: ($220,000-100,000/50,000) |

You can see why investors borrow. They are able to generate a higher rate of return by using debt when prices increase. Instead of a 12% annual return, the use of debt allows them to achieve a 24% annual return, and that has a substantial positive impact on one's ability to create wealth.

But, let's see what happens if instead of increasing in value, the asset declines in price by 30% over 10 years:

| | |
|---|---|
| **Original investment:** | $50,000 |
| **Add debt used:** | $50,000 (50% leverage ratio) |
| **Total investment:** | $100,000 |
| **Asset value 10 years later:** | $70,000 |
| **10-year rate of return without debt:** | -30%: ($70,000-$100,000)/$100,000 |
| **10-year rate of return with debt:** | -60%: ($70,000-100,000/50,000) |

The chart to the left shows examples of how the use of debt can have either a positive or negative multiplier effect. Note that when the asset increases in value, the use of debt leads to a higher rate of return, a good thing. However, when the asset declines in value, the rate of return is much worse when debt is used. Worse yet, what if you don't have the money to pay the bank its $50,000 back? Did your contract give them the right to foreclose on your home? Attach a lien to other assets? Garnish wages? Playing with debt is playing with fire. It can be used for good, but it can get out of control all too quickly and with serious consequences.

It's a sad fact: Because of the possibility of generating "oversize" positive returns, people are often tempted to use more debt than they should. The old saying "If a little is good, more must be better" does not often apply when it comes to debt. When borrowing for productive purposes, you want to keep the "loan-to-value" ratio (the amount borrowed in relation to the value of the asset purchased) reasonable and make sure you have adequate liquidity to withstand an economic slump.

You'll also want to carefully consider how much risk you are willing to take, and if you are married this discussion must include your spouse. Are you willing to have your home or children's college funds used as collateral for the loan? In most cases, I recommend that collateral be limited to the asset being financed so that personal exposure is limited. In other words, if you buy a car, and then through some misfortune default on the loan, the car should be the collateral, not the car *and* your bike *and* your entire iTunes library. If the only way you can obtain a loan is to use your home or other "committed" assets as collateral, I recommend you avoid taking out such a loan.

## Get-Rich-Quick Schemes

Who hasn't found themselves a little sheepish after signing up for that mail-order program that was supposed to make you a millionaire in two weeks but only left you twenty dollars poorer? Okay, maybe not everyone is gullible enough to do that, but plenty of us are, and no one is exempt from the risk of being taken in by business or investment opportunities that seem too good to pass up. Don't let this take you by surprise. The Catechism reminds us that "Our thirst for another's goods is immense, infinite, never quenched." (CCC

2536) This thirst for wealth makes us vulnerable to the many frauds promoted today.

A sadly ironic aspect of investment scams is that it is often those who can least afford to lose the money who fall prey. I recently received a letter from one such family. In a tight financial situation with mounting credit card bills, the wife heard about an opportunity for a home-based business that would allow her to stay home with their children while generating sufficient income to pay down their debts. The required start-up fee was a whopping $12,000, plus equipment and training to the tune of another $4,000. Since the couple had no savings, these charges went right onto credit cards.

You can guess what happened. After taking the money from who knows how many people, the operators are nowhere to be found. Now this family, which already had credit card problems, has added thousands of dollars more to their debt. There is no happy ending to this episode of the family's financial life.

How can you avoid making the same costly mistake?

☾ Don't fall into the trap of seeking quick riches. In Proverbs 13:11, we read, "Wealth hastily gotten will dwindle, but he who gathers little by little will increase it."

☾ Take time to research any investment adequately before you hand over funds. Proverbs 21:5 says, "The plans of the diligent lead surely to abundance, but everyone who is hasty comes only to want." In other words, if it sounds too

good to be true . . . you know the rest.

☾ Consider good counsel the twin of solid research—especially the counsel of your spouse. Make a point to seek it.

☾ Don't borrow money to invest unless there is a guaranteed method of repayment.

For many of you, this will be the first time you have heard many of these concepts. That's okay. What is important is that you appreciate and understand a few principles that will enable you to create the wealth you need to fulfill the responsibilities the Lord entrusts to you. Using your time and talent to create wealth and use it responsibly is part of what being a steward of Providence is all about.

## Discussion Topics

Read the discussion topic questions and write down your thoughts. This should be done prior to your class or small group get-together. In your class or small group, you'll share your thoughts with each other. For those discussion topics that list a Bible or Catechism reference, review it by referring to the applicable text at the beginning of the session.

## Discussion Topic 1
## Catechism 2404, Matthew 25:20–21, Matthew 6:24, Mark 8:36, Luke 12:16–21

Describe a Catholic understanding of how wealth should be viewed.
What responsibility do we have to create wealth? How should it be used?

_____

_____

_____

_____

_____

_____

_____

_____

_____

_____

## Discussion Topic 2

Describe why saving early and consistently is important. How does the rate of return impact your ability to create wealth? What benefit does an asset allocation and rebalancing approach to managing your investments provide?

_____

_____

_____

_____

_____

_____

_____

_____

_____

_____

_____

## Activity

Follow the instructions of your teacher/leader as he (or she) guides you through this session's activity. The activity is designed to help you apply the concepts learned in this session in a fun and engaging way.

Session Six

# Understanding and Managing Debt

## Session Objectives

◌ Learn what the Bible and Catechism say about debt.

◌ Recognize the difference between productive and unproductive debt.

◌ Understand how to eliminate unproductive debt using the Accelerator Repayment Plan.

## Key Terms

Productive Debt

Appreciating Asset

Depreciating Asset

Annual Percentage Interest Rate

Debit Card

Accelerator Repayment Plan

Unproductive Debt

Income-Producing Asset

Amortization

Minimum Payment

Credit Card

## Bible and Catechism References

Deuteronomy 15:5-6: "[I]f only you will obey the voice of the Lord your God, being careful to do all this commandment which I command you this day. For the Lord your God will bless you, as he promised you, and you shall lend to many nations, but you shall not borrow; and you shall rule over many nations, but they shall not rule over you."

Proverbs 22:7: "[T]he borrower is the slave of the lender."

Proverbs 22:26-27: "Be not one of those who give pledges, who become surety for debts. If you have nothing with which to pay, why should your bed be taken from under you?"

Habakkuk 2:6-7: "'Woe to him who heaps up what is not his own—for how long?—and loads himself with pledges!' Will not your debtors suddenly arise, and those awake who will make you tremble?"

Romans 13:8: "Owe no one anything, except to love one another; for he who loves his neighbor has fulfilled the law."

Catechism 2410-2411: "Promises must be kept and contracts strictly observed to the extent that the commitments made in them are morally just. . . . Contracts are subject to commutative justice which regulates exchanges between persons and between institutions in accordance with a strict respect for their rights. Commutative justice obliges strictly; it requires safeguarding property rights, paying debts, and fulfilling obligations freely contracted."

Psalms 37:21: "The wicked borrows, and cannot pay back, but the righteous is generous and gives."

Proverbs 6:1–5: "My son, if you have become surety for your neighbor, have given your pledge for a stranger; if you are snared in the utterance of your lips, caught in the words of your mouth; then do this, my son, and save yourself, for you have come into your neighbor's power: go, hasten, and importune your neighbor. Give your eyes no sleep and your eyelids no slumber; save yourself like a gazelle from the hunter, like a bird from the hand of the fowler."

# Reading

My oldest son is a fun-loving, outgoing young man. He enjoys life. As a young teen, he would always ooh and aah when he saw a fancy car or boat. Given his outgoing nature, Chelsey and I knew we would find it a challenge to help him understand the ramifications of borrowing, the need to save for the future, and how to prioritize current spending. Money burned a hole in his pocket. He was the type of person who had spent all his money (at least in his mind) even before he earned it!

I knew we had made progress when one day, as we were driving to a friend's house, he saw a beautiful boat in a front yard. I was expecting the typical, "Wow, what a cool boat" comment. Instead, he blurted out, "I wonder how much debt they're in!" My smile, I must admit, was pretty wide. He was beginning to realize that while, yes, the boat was pretty cool, there are often strings attached that an outsider doesn't know about. Often, things aren't as they appear.

In this session, we're going to discuss one of the most important financial issues of our day— the proper understanding and management of debt. Through the misuse of debt, many are forever kept from financial freedom, or find it only after climbing an incredibly rocky and steep road out of the debt pit.

I don't want this to happen to you.

Once you understand Catholic sensibilities about debt, its basic economics, and how debt and human behavior interact, you'll be equipped to manage debt well. Additional debt topics will be discussed in the sessions on creating wealth and being a savvy consumer.

## The History of Consumer Credit

Prior to the twentieth century, what we think of today as "consumer credit" didn't exist. Borrowing and lending occurred (after all, it's written about in the Bible), but it was on a much more limited scale, and was much more personal.

Early in the twentieth century, hotels and gasoline companies began issuing "charge cards" to their best customers. This wasn't credit as we think of it today. Any balances built up over the course of a month needed to be paid in full at the end of the month. It wasn't long before retailers like Spiegel House Furnishings Company, Sears Roebuck, and Montgomery Ward began to see the potential benefits of offering "installment sales," another precursor of the consumer credit we have today. Installment sales were typically offered on "big ticket" items like furniture. You simply made a small down payment and regular "small" monthly payments over time. But you got to enjoy the furniture right away. Pretty tempting!

Why was this such a great deal for the retailers? Two reasons. First, since buyers didn't have to come up with all the cash at once, they sold more product. Second, they made money on the interest they charged. In our day, it's not uncommon for the finance arms of manufacturers and retailers to be major profit centers. From installment sales, consumer credit has evolved to a sophisticated multibillion-dollar industry.

Consumer credit may be good for the banks and credit card companies, but it's not so good for you. Why not? Let's start our answer to that by learning what the Bible and Church have to say about debt.

## What Do the Bible and Catechism Say about Debt?

To hear how our grandparents and great grandparents speak about debt, you might come away thinking that it is sinful to borrow. Is it? Well, not quite. There are a number of references to debt in the Bible, and although they don't describe borrowing as a sin, they do speak of the negative consequences associated with debt. They encourage caution. It's this sense of caution that previous generations have tried to pass on to succeeding generations. But we haven't been listening so well.

Our Lord even speaks about debt at the national level. When speaking to the Israelites in the Old Testament, the Lord listed a number of blessings the Israelite people would enjoy by faithfully following him. One of those blessings had to do with debt. He said, "[I]f only you will obey the voice of the Lord your God, being careful to do all this commandment which I command you this day. For the Lord your God will bless you, as he promised you, and you shall lend to many nations, but you shall not borrow; and you shall rule over many nations, but they shall not rule over you." (Deut. 15:5–6)

The Lord is expressing a recurring theme: Borrowers don't control their own destiny. In some manner or other, they will be "ruled" by the lender. This same theme applies to the personal level as well. Proverbs 22:7 says, "[T]he borrower is the slave of the lender." Borrowing by its nature, brings with it a sense of bondage. It's easy to get into debt, but not so easy to get out.

Proverbs 22:26—27 speaks of the real-life consequences of not being able to pay one's debts. It says, "Be not one of those who give pledges, who become surety for debts. If you have nothing with which to pay, why should your bed be taken from under you?" Every day in America, people who have overcommitted themselves have their homes foreclosed on or their cars repossessed.

So, at a minimum, we should have a very cautious attitude toward debt. Debt isn't inherently sinful, but can you think of an example when it could be?

Let me share a true story with you. A woman owned a number of rental properties. She had lost most of her tenants, who had damaged the rental homes when they left. She needed to repair the damages before she could rent the homes again, but she didn't have the money. A "friend" suggested she pay for the repairs with her credit card, default on the balance, and negotiate with the creditors to settle the debt for cents on the dollar. Would that be sinful? In all likelihood, yes.

It's one thing to find yourself in over your head financially while having every intent to repay. It's quite another to enter into a transaction with no intent to repay. Here is what the Catechism says: "Promises must be kept and contracts strictly observed to the extent that the commitments made in them are morally just. . . . Contracts are subject to commutative justice which regulates exchanges between persons and between institutions in accordance with a strict respect for their rights. Commutative justice obliges strictly; it requires safeguarding property rights, paying debts, and fulfilling obligations freely contracted." (CCC 2410–2411) Psalm 37:21 is harsher yet: "The wicked borrows, and cannot pay back."

Take seriously the charge to develop the type of cautious attitude toward debt that Scripture and Church teaching encourage us to have. When used prudently, debt can help you reach your financial goals. When used imprudently, it can be a source of financial ruin. How can you tell the difference between productive and unproductive use of debt? That's an important question, but before it can be answered, you need to understand the session's key terms. Take a moment now to review the key term definitions in the Appendix.

Given the general rule of thumb that debt is productive when it is used prudently to purchase an appreciating and/or income-producing asset, and that it is unproductive when it is used to purchase depreciating assets, let's consider several types of purchases people make using debt to see whether it is being used productively or unproductively.

## Credit Card Debt: Productive or Unproductive?

Think of how people use credit cards. Do they use them to purchase assets that appreciate in value or produce income? Hardly. People buy things like groceries, gas, and entertainment, all of which are consumables. These depreciate in value—and fast. And if you carry a balance from month to month, the interest rates are very high. Carrying a balance on credit cards is always unproductive. It's a lose/lose proposition. Don't go there.

Here is an example of how this works. A credit card statement shows a balance of $2,442.46. The finance company requires that only $49.00 be paid to keep the account current. How long will it take (the amortization period) to pay down the debt? Sixteen years! What's the annual percentage interest rate? 15.24%, and that's if you are a good credit risk. How much interest will be paid during those 16 years? $5,071! Do you really want to pay over $7,500 for pizza and other consumables? I doubt it. Unfortunately, many people fall into this trap, and often for much more than two or three thousand dollars.

Let's look at this another way. What would happen if you invested the $2,442 today and each year added $316.93 to that investment (the amount of interest you'd otherwise pay to the finance company) and earned 8% each year on your invested funds? In sixteen years, the balance would grow to $18,748! Wouldn't you rather have your money working for you than against you?

Just because it doesn't make sense to carry a balance on a credit card doesn't mean they can't be used at all. It's certainly convenient to pay for items electronically, and electronic payment options include debit and credit cards. Debit cards are the safer bet for avoiding credit problems. But if you have good financial discipline, credit cards do offer a few benefits, including greater recourse in the event of a dispute with a vendor and attractive customer incentive programs. But these are only worthwhile if you aren't getting into debt and paying heavy interest charges. Credit cards are only productive when they are used to purchase items that are part of your spending plan and are paid in full at the end of each billing cycle.

## Home Loans: Productive or Unproductive?

One of the most common uses of debt is the purchase of a home with a mortgage. Is it productive to borrow to purchase your home? In general, yes. Of course, each situation is unique. But assuming you'll be in the home for a long period of time, you can expect prices to increase at about the rate of inflation. That doesn't mean your price can't go down. It's not unusual for parts of the country to experience price bubbles that eventually burst. But again, over decades, housing prices have tended to increase at about the same pace as general inflation. Look for more on this in the sessions on creating wealth and real estate.

## Student Loans: Productive or Unproductive?

What about student loans? Are they productive or unproductive? This gets a bit more subjective, but to the extent that they increase your capacity to earn income, they can be productive. It's all a function of how much debt you are taking on and how much your earnings potential is being increased. That's not to say there aren't other valuable reasons to get a college education, especially in a Catholic environment. But you'll want to weigh very carefully how much debt you'll leave college with.

Once, when I was a guest on a radio show, a woman called in and said her daughter had been admitted to the most prestigious music school in the country. The four-year education was expected to cost $250,000 and the school was not offering any scholarship funds. The caller asked my advice. Although the daughter obviously had great talent, the probability of earning a substantial income as a performer was very small. I suggested she consider applying to other well-respected music schools where she could be expected to receive substantial scholarship funds—and potentially a complete scholarship. The woman was perturbed by my suggestion

and asked how I could limit her daughter's potential in this way.

None of us wants to "limit" anyone's potential, but it's a fact that we need to do the best we can given finite resources. Funding for college should be a partnership between the student, the parents, and the school. Although borrowing for college can be productive, students and parents need to be realistic about the full amount that will be borrowed and the ramifications left by such debt after graduation.

## Automobile Loans: Productive or Unproductive?

Do cars appreciate in value? Some classic and antique cars will increase in value, but the vast majority of automobiles decline in value. In fact, it's not uncommon for a new car to depreciate fifteen percent once you drive it off the lot! Yet, the vast majority of Americans borrow to purchase their cars. It wasn't always this way. Just ask your grandparents.

Borrowing to purchase a car often leads to buying more car than is needed or than one can afford. In an effort to clinch the sale, the sales rep will entice you with offers of no down payment and small monthly payments. Don't be fooled. With few exceptions, you are better off saving ahead of time rather than borrowing to buy a car.

## Home Equity Loans: Productive or Unproductive?

Home equity loans provide homeowners access to the equity, or the value of their home that exceeds the mortgage. Does it make sense to borrow against the value of your home? Although it depends on the proposed use of the borrowed funds, there are very few situations in which these funds are used to purchase an appreciating asset. Yet, people do it all the time for a variety of reasons: to make home improvements, to pay off credit card debt, to take a vacation, to buy a car or recreational vehicle, or to purchase rental properties.

Very few home improvements appreciate in value. They add value to the home, but typically far less than the amount borrowed and spent. People will make the argument that it's better to pay off unproductive credit card debt through a home equity loan. The benefits include deductibility of interest expense for taxes and lower interest rates. However, what people don't realize is that they are turning what should be short-term debt into long-term debt, and even with reduced interest rates, they will spend more than if they used the Accelerator Repayment Plan to pay down their credit card debt. The same is true for using home equity to buy vacations or recreational vehicles.

Vacations, though wonderful, don't retain any monetary value, and recreational vehicles depreciate more rapidly than cars.

Some people choose to borrow against the equity in their home in order to make an investment in which the rate of return can be expected to be greater than the interest rate on the loan. Examples include purchasing a rental property or starting a business. However, one needs to recognize the risk associated with such a loan. While some have created wealth with this approach, others have lost their homes. In general, I prefer not to consider my home as a source of investment capital.

As you can see, it really doesn't make sense to borrow against the hard-earned (sweat) equity in your home. We'll discuss whether it makes sense to borrow for business or investment purposes more generally in the session on creating wealth.

# Accelerator Repayment Plan Example

| Owed to | Balance | Rate | Minimum Monthly Payment | # of Payments Based on Minimum Payment | # of Payments Based on Accelerator Plan |
|---|---|---|---|---|---|
| **Visa** | 4,000 | 19% | $120 | 48 | 14 payments at $330 |
| **Discover** | 2,000 | 17% | $60 | 46 | 14 payments at $60 and 4 payments at $390 |
| **MasterCard** | 4,000 | 14% | 110 | 48 | 18 payments at $110 and 6 payments at $500 |
| **Car Loan** | 10,000 | 8% | $300 | 38 | 24 payments at $300 and 5 payments at $800 |
| **Totals** | 20,000 | NA | $590 | NA | NA |

## Eliminating Unproductive Debt: The Accelerator Repayment Plan

If someone accumulates unproductive debt, it is a good idea to eliminate that debt as soon as possible using what I call the Accelerator Repayment Plan. It is a common financial approach to eliminating debt in typically less than half the time it would otherwise take.

In the example to the left, a couple has three credit cards with balances totaling $10,000 and a car loan for $10,000. The minimum monthly payments total $590. If they continue to make the minimum payments, it would take about four years to become debt free. What could they do differently?

Rather than focus on making the minimum payment, the Accelerator Repayment Plan recognizes the financial damage being done by paying high levels of interest, and applies the resources necessary to eliminate the debt more quickly. In the example, if instead of paying the minimum, the couple applied $800 each month, the debt would be eliminated in less than two-and-a-half years.

You'll notice that the Accelerator Repayment Plan requires that you prioritize your debts for repayment. My preference is to pay the debts with the highest interest rate first. Paying these first will save the most money. Some people prefer to pay down the smallest debt first. The quick elimination of even a small debt gives a sense of achievement. Either way works, but the interest rate method yields the greatest savings.

Here's how the accelerator method works. Each month the borrower makes the minimum payment required on each of the loans, except for the loan at the top of the repayment list. This is the one being accelerated. In the example above, the minimum payment on the Visa bill is $120, but because the couple has committed $800 per month ($210 more than the minimum payment required on all loans), they can apply the additional $210 each month to the Visa card, for a total of $330.

When the Visa bill is paid off, almost three years ahead of time, they'll continue to apply $800 each month to the other outstanding debts. With the Visa bill gone, they can zero-in on the Discover Card. By adding the $330 payment they were making on the Visa bill to the $60 minimum payment they're making on the Discover Card, they make a payment of $390. You can see how that amount will pay off the Discover Card in no time. Borrowers can repeat this process until the debts are eliminated!

The best thing is that once you are debt free, you now have the $800 each month to use for much better purposes than paying off debts. If you saved and invested the $800 every month at 8%, in fifteen years you would have over $279,000. If you kept investing it for an additional twenty years, your balance would grow to more than $1.8 million. What a difference being free of debt makes! Of course, the $800 doesn't come out of thin air. You have to reprioritize your spending or create additional income to make the plan work, but the benefits are worth the effort.

## Debt: Family and Friends

The final topic for this session relates to debts between family and friends. Why do I bring this up? Because debt between family and friends has a way of changing the underlying relationship—often in harmful ways.

Here is what Scripture says: "My son, if you have become surety for your neighbor, have given your pledge for a stranger; if you are snared in the utterance of your lips, caught in the words of your mouth; then do this, my son, and save yourself, for you have come into your neighbor's power: go, hasten, and importune your neighbor. Give your eyes no sleep and your eyelids no slumber; save yourself like a gazelle from the hunter, like a bird from the hand of the fowler." (Proverbs 6:1–5)

Debt creates expectations and burdens. Even if an arrangement is entered into with the best intentions, circumstances change. Miscommunications and misunderstandings are common. Think twice before borrowing from or lending to family and friends, including co-signing on loans. If a situation arises in which you or family members need help, it may be better to make an outright gift rather than a loan, with the inherent relationship complications.

## Discussion Topics

Read the discussion topic questions and write down your thoughts. This should be done prior to your class or small group get-together. In your class or small group, you'll share your thoughts with each other. For those discussion topics that list a Bible or Catechism reference, review it by referring to the applicable text at the beginning of the session.

## Discussion Topic 1
## Proverbs 22:7

Proverbs 22:7 compares owing money to being a slave. List five ways that your life is impacted negatively when you owe someone money.

_____

_____

_____

_____

_____

_____

_____

_____

_____

_____

## Discussion Topic 2

List five examples in which debt could be used productively and five examples where the use of debt would be unproductive. Describe the consequences of borrowing unproductively.

_____

_____

_____

_____

_____

_____

_____

_____

_____

_____

## Activity

Follow the instructions of your teacher/leader as he (or she) guides you through this session's activity. The activity is designed to help you apply the concepts learned in this session in a fun and engaging way.

Session Seven

# Marriage and Money

## Session Objectives

   *Ó*  Understand the impact that money issues have on marriage.

   *Ó*  Recognize the importance of fostering unity in marriage.

   *Ó*  Realize the importance of honesty, good communication, and counsel when it comes to managing money in marriage.

   *Ó*  Learn how to assess talents in marriage and to divide responsibilities.

   *Ó*  Learn financial tips as you prepare for marriage.

## Key Terms

| | | |
|---|---|---|
| Marriage | Unity | Honesty |
| Counsel | Talents | Family Budget Meeting |
| Pre-existing Debt | Combined Financial Plan | Joint Checking Account |

## Bible and Catechism References

Catechism 1660: "The marriage covenant, by which a man and a woman form with each other an intimate communion of life and love, has been founded and endowed with its own special laws by the Creator. By its very nature it is ordered to the good of the couple, as well as to the generation and education of children. Christ the Lord raised marriage between the baptized to the dignity of a sacrament."

Genesis 2:24: "Therefore a man leaves his father and mother and clings to his wife, and they become one flesh."

Proverbs 15:22: "Without counsel plans go wrong, but with many advisers they succeed."

John 8:44: "When he [satan] lies, he speaks according to his own nature, for he is a liar and the father of lies."

Catechism 2464: "The eighth commandment forbids misrepresenting the truth in our relations with others. This moral prescription flows from the vocation of the holy people to bear witness to their God who is the truth and wills the truth. Offenses against the truth express by word or deed a refusal to commit oneself to moral uprightness: they are fundamental infidelities to God and, in this sense, they undermine the foundations of the covenant."

1 Corinthians 12:4-7: "Now there are varieties of gifts, but the same Spirit; and there are varieties of service, but the same Lord; and there are varieties of working, but it is the same God who inspires them all in every one. To each is given the manifestation of the Spirit for the common good."

# Reading

Practically everyone has something to say about marriage. When it comes to this topic, I get a kick out of the advice given by young people. Here are a few snippets:

Alan (age 10) was asked, "How do you decide who to marry?" His answer?

"You got to find somebody who likes the same stuff. Like, if you like sports, she should like it that you like sports, and she should keep the chips and dip coming."

When asked, "Is it better to be single or married?" Anita (age 9) responded:

> "It's better for girls to be single, but not for boys. Boys need someone to clean up after them."

*Ouch.* Finally, the coup de grace. Ricky (age 10) was asked how to make a marriage work. He replied:

> "Tell your wife that she looks pretty, even if she looks like a truck."

That's the wisdom of the very young. What does the Church say about marriage?

> "The marriage covenant, by which a man and a woman form with each other an intimate communion of life and love, has been founded and endowed with its own special laws by the Creator. By its very nature it is ordered to the good of the couple, as well as to the generation and education of children. Christ the Lord raised marriage between the baptized to the dignity of a sacrament." (CCC 1660)

God dreamed up marriage as pretty exciting stuff. Adam and Eve enjoyed a blissful union until they messed up by biting into that apple. We know this isn't any Garden of Eden anymore. But when Jesus died on the cross, he gave men and women a new possibility of true union. Although this union is, of course, about a lot more than money, money impacts every marriage in ways that might surprise you. How? The way we manage our money reflects who we are as people. Think about that for a moment. When you know a person's money habits, you know a lot about what makes him tick.

You probably know that half of all marriages end in divorce. What you may not know is that money issues are one of the primary causes of divorce. With this sorry statistic in mind, it is a gift to learn a God-centered approach to managing money before you get married. So often when I'm visiting with an older couple, they'll say, "We wish we had known about this twenty years ago!" You can know these things now. By learning and applying these principles today, you can avoid making mistakes that stick with people for a lifetime. Instead, you can set your marriage on a firm foundation.

## Marital Unity: Understanding Yourself, Understanding Your Spouse

The transition from life as a single person to life united to another is exciting. But that doesn't mean it's always easy. You are two different people who come from two different backgrounds. Yet, you are called to establish a union—as the Catechism said above, an "intimate communion of life and love."

Here's how Genesis 2:24 describes it: "Therefore a man leaves his father and mother and clings to his wife, and they become one flesh." You can see that this refers to the physical union that takes place in marriage, which is a great gift, but the physical union expresses an even deeper union, the union on the level of the soul. When we marry someone, we marry the whole person, body and soul.

Did you notice in the Genesis verse that leaving comes before cleaving? It's surprising how few couples understand the need to leave their parents by making a healthy break as they begin their journey. It's not that you don't continue to love your parents and remain involved with your family, but something needs to change. You and your spouse need to establish your own life together. Let me share a couple of stories to shed more light on this issue.

Bill and Sue both came from solid Catholic families. Both had hardworking fathers, but Sue's father was a physician and brought home a much bigger paycheck than Bill's father did. After Bill and Sue got married, Bill started his career in sales. He was good at his work, and his future looked promising, but there was less money coming in during those beginning days than Sue was used to. A change in lifestyle was needed. Did Sue make that change? She didn't, and the cost was mounting credit card debt and tension in the relationship. Sue hadn't successfully navigated the leaving part of Genesis 2:24.

Chris and Mary both grew up in households with very modest incomes, and although they had loving parents who worked hard to insure their basic needs were met, many wants went unmet.

Chris and Mary wanted to give their children all the things they didn't get when they were young. So, when house prices bubbled in their area, they borrowed in excess of $100,000 against the value of their house through home equity loans. With the borrowed money, they bought all types of goodies, including new home furnishings, an RV, and Sea-Doos. While it was fun for a while, eventually the housing bubble burst and they found themselves owing more than their house was worth.

These young couples made money decisions based on their experiences growing up rather than on a core set of principles. As a result, the debt they created would take many years to overcome, impacting their relationship and their ability to reach their future goals.

How can you avoid making the same mistakes? You need to understand yourselves and each other—what makes you tick and why—and you need to place Christ at the center of your relationship. Let's touch on each of these points.

Do you recall the heritage question I posed in Session One? How your parents think about money, communicate about it, and have managed it over the years is bound to have a substantial impact on how you do those things today. The same holds true for your future spouse.

Backgrounds are often different, and it takes time to get on the same page. But doing so is a key to succeeding in marriage. That is why I encourage all couples preparing for marriage to discuss the heritage question with each other during the courtship phase of their relationship. It is a start toward establishing the unity that is vital to their marriage.

Now, recall the discussion we had on Money Personality Types. Just as with the heritage question, knowing your own and your future spouse's money personality type will be a key to unlocking your natural inclinations when it comes to money. Are you a saver or a spender? Free-spirited or disciplined and organized? How does your personality type compare to your future spouse's? Don't worry—differences in personality types are often a good thing. The world could get boring pretty quickly if we were all the same. But recognizing that your core personality traits will have a major influence on how you think about money and act with it is important. Make sure to discuss your money personality types during your dating years.

## Christ in the Middle

Even though you come from different backgrounds and have different money personality types, in marriage you have a common goal. That goal is to help each other and your children reach heaven. With Christ at the center of your relationship, you can reach that goal. Even when you're starting from different places, if Christ is in the middle and you are growing closer to him, then by default you will be growing closer to each other. How do you do this? By making the spiritual plan described in Session Three a part of your life as a couple.

## The Importance of Honesty

God "is the truth and wills the truth." (CCC 2464) John the apostle describes Satan as having "nothing to do with the truth, because there is no truth in him. When he lies, he speaks according to his own nature, for he is a liar and the father of lies." (John 8:44)

Given these descriptions, do you think a marriage can withstand a lack of honesty? It makes it pretty tough, especially when it becomes a pattern. Yet, money matters are an area prone to dishonesty between spouses, ranging from a general lack of openness to outright lying.

But even when bad patterns have been established, there is hope for the future. I remember working with a couple who had gotten into a tight financial spot. The husband was a hard worker, but revealed that over the years he hadn't been the steward of Providence he should have been. He had made a number of financial mistakes that caused him embarrassment. In an attempt to set things right, he began taking all the family's financial paperwork to his workplace, leaving his wife completely in the dark about their situation. It was only after he began to understand what it means to manage money based on Christian principles that he realized the mistake he had made by not being open with his wife. Since then, they have developed a team approach to managing their money.

## The Importance of Counsel

Counsel is also an important scriptural principle. The Bible has a lot to say about counsel. Who should be your primary counselor? In marriage, many people assume it should be their spouse. But there is a counselor even more important than your husband or wife—the One who made you.

Psalm 32:8 says, "I will instruct you and teach you the way you should go; I will counsel you with my eye upon you." Why is it important for God to be our primary counselor? As important as one's spouse, friends, and professional advisors are, they're more or less in the same boat of human imperfection that you are. God alone has all the answers. How can you know his counsel? By knowing him well. That means making him part of every day through prayer and the other parts of the spiritual plan discussed in Session Three.

Just because the Lord should be your primary counselor doesn't mean you shouldn't turn to others for advice as well. In fact, he encourages it. Proverbs 15:22 says, "Without counsel plans go wrong, but with many advisers they succeed." And Proverbs 11:14 tells us, "For lack of guidance a people falls; security lies in many counselors."

It's appropriate that, after God, your spouse should be the counselor of greatest importance to you. Beyond your spouse you'll want to seek the counsel of family, friends, spiritual directors, and professional advisors. A good counselor won't threaten the marital relationship. When the two of you turn together to a well-chosen third party, it should strengthen your union as a couple.

A word here about the necessity of receiving wise and godly counsel. The prophet Isaiah speaks of ungodly counsel in the following way: "But when I look there is no one; among them there is no counselor who, when I ask, gives an answer. Behold, they are all a delusion; their works are nothing; their molten images are empty wind!" (Is. 41:28–29)."

Choose your counselors carefully. A poor counselor can easily do more harm than good. In fact, St. Paul says, "Do not be deceived: 'Bad company corrupts good morals'" (1 Cor. 15:33).

Whether you are developing plans for the future or find yourself in the middle of a sticky situation today, make sure to seek the counsel of the Lord and the wise people he has placed around you.

## Financial To-Do's before Marriage

As you prepare for marriage, it will be important to address some key financial issues. An ounce of prevention is worth a pound of cure. It's better to think these issues through during the months leading up to your marriage than to wait until the ring is on your finger.

## Who Will Handle the Details? Assessing Your Talents

When I counsel married couples, one of the big topics we address is who handles the day-to-day financial issues, like setting up a budget, paying bills, and tracking income and expenses. When I ask the spouse handling these responsibilities how he ended up with the job, it's not unusual for him to say, "Because that's the way Mom and Dad always did it!"

Well, maybe that worked for Mom and Dad—and maybe it didn't. Instead of trying to stick a square peg into a round hole, it makes sense to assess who has the skill and attitude to manage the money basics. St. Paul wrote beautifully about how the Lord has distributed talents. He said:

"Now there are varieties of gifts, but the same Spirit; and there are varieties of service, but the same Lord; and there are varieties of working, but it is the same God who inspires them all in every one. To each is given the manifestation of the Spirit for the common good." (1 Cor. 12:4–7)

We all have talent. But none of us has every talent. Take me: On the one hand, I have a certain level of skill when it comes to managing money and organizing things. On the other hand, God saw fit to make me woefully deficient in the Mr.-Fix-It department. Put a wrench in my hand and you're really asking for trouble. When Chelsey and I saw a bumper sticker on a plumber's truck that said, "We repair what your husband fixed!" we knew who it was talking about!

God wants us to depend on each other. St. Paul says that by combining our talents, we can accomplish a greater good. That's true in marriage, and it's true in society as a whole.

Before determining who should handle the financial basics, think through who has the stronger administrative and math skills. That person should probably be the one handling the details. That may mean that other responsibilities need to be taken over by the other spouse, since managing money well takes a reasonable amount of time. Just because one spouse handles the financial details, does it mean that the other spouse is off the hook? Not if this is going to be a joint effort. One of the goals of the spouse handling the details is to prepare summary information

(using the tools learned in this program) that will help the couple assess where they are today, where they are going, and how to get there. Couples that make it a habit to communicate regularly about their finances are doing something smart. I call these get-togethers family budget meetings. It often works for couples to start out with little weekly meetings, graduating to monthly ones as they build solid habits.

## Dealing with Pre-existing Debts

Although I dealt with the topic of debt more fully in another session, I want to address the question of how to handle pre-existing debts that you and your future spouse carry with you into the marriage. There are ways to avoid legally marrying your future spouse's debts, but they require keeping your finances much more separated than is desirable in a marriage. It is my opinion that for all practical purposes you do marry your spouse's debts. So be prepared for it!

Before anything else, make sure you agree on what your attitude toward debt will be as a couple. I hope, that based on the materials in this program, you recognize the importance of having a cautious attitude toward all debt, while recognizing that debt can be used either productively or unproductively. To the extent you borrow as a couple, make sure that it is for productive purposes.

How much debt does each of you have? Use the Summary of Debts form (provided in the appendix) to get a clear picture of where you stand. What caused the debts? Are they productive or unproductive? Were they caused by lax spending habits? Have those habits been overcome or do they continue today?

If the debts were caused by bad spending habits, you need to have a serious discussion about whether those habits have been corrected or not. This sounds harsh, but I recommend that if bad habits have not changed, you hold off on making wedding plans until they have.

I remember a young woman whose fiancé had accumulated credit card debt as a result of habitual spending. She established the requirement that he eliminate his credit card debt before she would marry him. She knew that the discipline acquired through eliminating his debt would prove invaluable throughout their lives together, and that it was better he learned it now. He loved her enough to make that commitment. He banished his debt and won his beloved bride as a prize. That was one wise lady.

Use the Accelerator Repayment Plan to establish a game plan for eliminating your debt (especially unproductive debt) as quickly as possible. In some cases, it will be reasonable for the debt to carry over into the marriage. In others, as noted above, it may be best to eliminate the debt either entirely, or at least in part, before you get married.

## Setting Up Bank Accounts: Joint or Separate?

You'll want to set up your finances in such a way that facilitates achieving the marital unity spoken of earlier. That means you should have a combined

financial plan (budget) that reflects your combined resources and responsibilities. What does that mean by way of bank accounts?

There's no one way to do it, but I recommend that couples set up a joint checking account that is funded with both their salaries and other sources of income. The spouse paying the bills would pay from this account.

That doesn't mean there isn't room for additional separate accounts. Each of you may want to have an "allowance" checking account that is funded from your main checkbook. That allows you to budget for the allowances properly, but also provides flexibility for spending your allowance without too many strings attached. You'll want to use no-fee or low-fee accounts for these, otherwise the charges will chew up your allowances.

## Other Issues

Some people will already have a substantial financial life prior to getting married, either as a result of inheriting money or getting married later in life. It's a common practice in today's culture for couples to enter into prenuptial agreements. The problem with these is that they focus on what will happen in the event the marriage fails—not quite the attitude of trust you'd hope for between persons about to commit their lives to each other.

It is my belief that if you are not at the point where you can combine resources with your future spouse "for better or worse," then you aren't ready for marriage. In some cases, extenuating circumstances that warrant a prenuptial agreement may exist. For example, if one of you has dependents that rely on you for support and could be harmed in the event of a divorce, it may be a prudent action.

If your situation includes such complicating factors, you'll want to seek the counsel of professional advisers. But, you'll also want to be clear on the desire to establish an approach that builds the unity that is your ultimate objective.

## Discussion Topics

Read the discussion topic questions and write down your thoughts. This should be done prior to your class or small group get-together. In your class or small group, you'll share your thoughts with each other. For those discussion topics that list a Bible or Catechism reference, review it by referring to the applicable text at the beginning of the session.

## Discussion Topic 1

What can you learn about a person from his (or her) financial habits? How should couples determine which spouse should manage the financial details in the household?

_____

_____

_____

_____

_____

_____

_____

_____

_____

## Discussion Topic 2

Describe five ways family budget meetings can benefit both a marriage and a family's finances.

_____

_____

_____

_____

_____

_____

_____

_____

_____

_____

## Activity

Follow the instructions of your teacher/leader as he (or she) guides you through this session's activity. The activity is designed to help you apply the concepts learned in this session in a fun and engaging way.

Session Eight

# The Call to Generosity

## Session Objectives

Ⓞ Learn how generosity is described in sacred Scripture and what the Church teaches about it today.

Ⓞ Understand what it means to tithe and give from our "first fruits."

Ⓞ Understand how cultivating a generous spirit makes you a better person, enhancing your relationship with God and those around you.

Ⓞ Be equipped to make giving a core part of your financial life.

## Key Terms

Tithing          Legalistic          Scrupulous          First Fruits

## Bible and Catechism References

Leviticus 27:30: "'All the tithe of the land, whether of the seed of the land or of the fruit of the trees, is the Lord's; it is holy to the Lord.'"

Proverbs 3:9: "Honor the Lord with your substance and with the first fruits of all your produce."

Malachi 3:7-10: "From the days of your fathers you have turned aside from my statutes and have not kept them. Return to me, and I will return to you, says the Lord of hosts. But you say, 'How shall we return?' Will man rob God? Yet you are robbing me. But you say, 'How are we robbing thee?' In your tithes and offerings. You are cursed with a curse, for you are robbing me; the whole nation of you. Bring the full tithes into the storehouse, that there may be food in my house; and thereby put me to the test, says the Lord of hosts, if I will not open the windows of heaven for you and pour down for you an overflowing blessing."

Matthew 23:23: "Woe to you, scribes and Pharisees, hypocrites! For you tithe mint and dill and cummin, and have neglected the weightier matters of the law, justice and mercy and faith; these you ought to have done, without neglecting the others."

Matthew 25:35-40: "'. . . for I was hungry and you gave me food, I was thirsty and you gave me drink, I was a stranger and you welcomed me, I was naked and you clothed me, I was sick and you visited me, I was in prison and you came to me.' Then the righteous will answer him, 'Lord, when did we see thee hungry and feed thee, or thirsty and give thee drink? And when did we see thee a stranger and welcome thee, or naked and clothe thee? And when did we see thee sick or in prison and visit thee?' And the King will answer them, 'Truly, I say to you, as you did it to one of the least of these my brethren, you did it to me.'"

2 Corinthians 9:6–7: "The point is this: He who sows sparingly will also reap sparingly, and he who sows bountifully will also reap bountifully. Each one must do as he has made up his mind, not reluctantly or under compulsion, for God loves a cheerful giver."

St. Irenaeus (Office of Readings, Second Saturday in Ordinary Time): "Thus the people of Israel used to dedicate tithes of their possessions. But those who have been given freedom devote what they possess to the Lord's use. They give it all to him, not simply what is of lesser value, cheerfully and freely because they hope for greater things, like the widow who put into God's treasury her whole livelihood."

Code of Canon Law 222: "The Christian faithful are obliged to assist with the needs of the Church so that the Church has what is necessary for divine worship, for apostolic works and works of charity and for the decent sustenance of ministers. They are also obliged to . . . assist the poor from their own resources."

## Reading

If you are a pastor at a church in the Las Vegas Diocese, or in another area where gambling is prevalent, you have an interesting challenge when it comes to donations: casino chips in the collection basket. What's the parish to do? Leave it to the ever-resourceful Catholic spirit. The diocese has assigned a priest to go to each of the casinos and cash in the chips so that the parishes can deposit the corresponding cash into their bank accounts. You'll never guess the nickname of the priest. Go ahead, give it a shot. You can find the answer at the end of the session.

Since St. Paul instructs us to be "cheerful givers," it seems only appropriate to start this chapter with a bit of humor. That said,

though, the call to generosity is serious stuff according to Scripture and Church teaching. They make it clear that cultivating a generous spirit is a key part of our Christian walk. Yet, this area of Christian life can be misunderstood.

Statistics on giving reveal that Americans as a whole give about two percent of their income to charity. American Catholics, on average, give a little over one percent. How do those numbers compare to what's revealed in Scripture and what the Church teaches today?

The Bible describes an approach to giving called tithing. To tithe means literally to give a tenth, or ten percent, of your income. A little more than just one percent, isn't it? If you are a normal fallen human being, your first impulse might be to ask, "Well, so what? How can that affect me?"

Essentially, it affects you because the place that generosity plays in your life says a lot about your priorities. It says a lot about the place Jesus has in your life and about how you reflect him to those around you. Not convinced yet? Let's take a closer look at why cultivating a generous spirit is so important. You don't need to take my word for it. Take God's.

## Why We Give: Love of God . . .

During Old Testament times, the Israelites had a hot and cold relationship with the Lord. They were a fickle people. At one of their lowest points, the Lord sent the prophet Malachi to show the Israelites how far they had drifted from his ways and how they could return. They had fallen into many awful habits, including dishonoring the marriage covenant and not giving the Lord due worship. They had become a selfish people. Here is what Malachi said:

"From the days of your fathers you have turned aside from my statutes and have not kept them. Return to me, and I will return to you, says the Lord of hosts. But you say, 'How shall we return?' Will man rob God? Yet you are robbing me. But you say, 'How are we robbing thee?' In your tithes and offerings. You are cursed with a curse, for you are robbing me; the whole nation of you. Bring the full tithes into the storehouse, that there may be food in my house; and thereby put me to the test, says the Lord of hosts, if I will not open the windows of heaven for you and pour down for you an overflowing blessing." (Malachi 3:7–10)

"Return to me and I will return to you!" Those are strong words, and they are linked to being faithful in tithing. Why is generosity so important? Because it is a key to unlocking a deeper relationship with Christ. The Lord couldn't get much clearer: He tells us to put him to the test through tithing. He promises to pour down abundant blessings on those who do.

Warning: You may be getting excited about a notion referred to as the "prosperity gospel." In short, this idea takes Scripture to mean that we should give money to God because he'll give lots more of it back to us. Some TV preachers have made careers out of this. But that's not Catholic teaching. The blessings the Lord describes will be those things that lead us to our eventual goal of eternal life with him—of reaching heaven. Sometimes those will be material blessings and sometimes they will be spiritual blessings. Sometimes the blessings even come to us disguised as crosses.

Just as with the Israelites in the Old Testament, the primary reason we give today is love of God. I call it a recognition factor. It's a healthy way for us to remember God's primary place in our lives.

## . . . And Love of Neighbor

Another reason we give is love of neighbor. Here is what Jesus had to say to his disciples:

> ". . . for I was hungry and you gave me food, I was thirsty and you gave me drink, I was a stranger and you welcomed me, I was naked and you clothed me, I was sick and you visited me, I was in prison and you came to me." Then the righteous will answer him, 'Lord, when did we see thee hungry and feed thee, or thirsty and give thee drink? And when did we see thee a stranger and welcome thee, or naked and clothe thee? And when did we see thee sick or in prison and visit thee?' And the King will answer them, "Truly, I say to you, as you did it to one of the least of these my brethren, you did it to me." (Matt. 25:35–40)

When I read those words, I think of Blessed Mother Teresa of Calcutta, who became known worldwide for seeing Christ in the poorest of the poor and reaching out to them in whatever way she could to alleviate their suffering.

About the importance of giving, Mother Teresa once said, "Give until it hurts." That's an important principle. True love is sacrificial in nature. And giving is about love.

## How We Give

So, the primary reason we give is love. But how are we supposed to live this call to generosity in our lives practically speaking? Here is how the Church summarizes our responsibility:

> "The Christian faithful are obliged to assist with the needs of the Church so that the Church has what is necessary for divine worship, for apostolic works and works of charity and for the decent sustenance of ministers. They are also obliged to . . . assist the poor from their own resources." (CCL 222)

You'll notice that although the Church describes several activities that deserve our charity, it doesn't specify how much we should give. The tithe was taught in the Old Testament, but the Church has the right to change the amount she asks us to give, and today she has left that decision up to us. We certainly shouldn't be legalistic or scrupulous when it comes to our generosity, but we should look at the tithe as a guide that gives us a clue about what is a reasonable amount. The specifics of the tithe itself may have changed, but the reason God instituted it remain as important as ever. That includes learning to give from our "first fruits." What does that mean? Here is what Scripture says:

"Honor the Lord with your substance and with the first fruits of all your produce." (Proverbs 3:9)

Giving from our first fruits means that we give the first and best of our increase back to the Lord. Since Adam and Eve, we've gotten into the bad habit of giving our leftovers to God. Forget about it. They won't satisfy him.

I ask you: Is it a sacrifice to give one percent of your income away? In most cases, giving at this level is an afterthought. How do you feel when someone you care about gives you a gift that you know was just an afterthought? About as special as a sack of potatoes. Your appreciation for the gift is linked to how much love and effort was put into it. It's the same with God.

Now ask yourself, would it be a sacrifice if you gave ten percent of your income? For most people, that would reach the level of "giving until it hurts" that Mother Teresa spoke about. Voila! Now you can understand the relevance of the 10% figure, even for today.

The following table shows the difference between giving one percent and ten percent at different income levels. It helps you visualize how the average American gives as an afterthought rather than making giving a planned part of their financial life in thanksgiving to God for the many gifts he has given to them.

# Giving Comparison—1 Percent/10 Percent

| Annual Income | Annual Giving at 1% | Annual Giving at 10% (Tithe) | Monthly Tithe |
|---|---|---|---|
| **$30,000** | $300 | $3,000 | $250 |
| **$40,000** | $400 | $4,000 | $333 |
| **$50,000** | $500 | $5,000 | $417 |
| **$75,000** | $750 | $7,500 | $625 |
| **$90,000** | $900 | $9,000 | $750 |
| **$120,000** | $1200 | $12,000 | $1,000 |

## Trusting in God's Providence

Living out the call to generosity involves growing in faith and learning to trust in God. There are a number of powerful examples in Scripture that teach us about this type of trust. The first two are similar. In 1 Kings 17:7–16, God instructs Elijah to go on a journey to Zar'ephath, where a widow will feed him. Upon reaching the town, Elijah sees the widow and asks for some bread. She lets him know she is preparing a final meal made from her last bit of food to share with her son, after which she expects them both to die. Elijah persists in his request and the woman at last offers him the meal she had intended for herself and her son. The result? A little Old Testament magic. They were able to eat for many days as the flour and oil miraculously continued to pour out. Other miraculous events include the story of Elisha and the widow in 2 Kings 4:1–7 and the multiplication of the fish and loaves in Matthew 14:13–21.

I don't mention these stories, of course, to set you up to expect financial miracles of the same sort, but to foster a sense of trust in God. "Phil, God's pretty big," a friend of mine once told me. God knows and wants what is best for us, and he wants each of us to stretch ourselves as we learn to be a truly generous person.

I will close with the story of a woman who called me some time ago. She thanked me for my work and told me that while she had wanted to start tithing, her husband hadn't been on the same page until he read some of my writings. Once he was convinced, they increased their giving, and she wanted to let me know that she had noticed changes in him. He had grown closer to God, to her, and to their children. That's what the call to generosity is all about.

So even though tithing, or giving ten percent, is not a requirement of the Church today, consider your obligation to be generous as described in the Code of Canon Law 222. Give tithing a try (as the Lord told us in Malachi 3:10), and see what blessings he has in store for you. Tithing is just the kind of cure our poor consumer-oriented culture needs to help it turn its heart back to God, one person at a time.

*Answer to joke at opening of chapter: Chip Monk.*

## Discussion Topics

Read the discussion topic questions and write down your thoughts. This should be done prior to your class or small group get-together. In your class or small group, you'll share your thoughts with each other. For those discussion topics that list a Bible or Catechism reference, review it by referring to the applicable text at the beginning of the session.

## Discussion Topic 1

Reread all the Scripture references listed at the beginning of the session.
Describe in your own words why it's important to cultivate a generous spirit.

_____

_____

_____

_____

_____

_____

_____

_____

_____

_____

_____

## Discussion Topic 2

List five concrete steps you can take to make giving a regular part of your financial life.

_____

_____

_____

_____

_____

_____

_____

_____

_____

_____

## Activity

Follow the instructions of your teacher/leader as he (or she) guides you through this session's activity. The activity is designed to help you apply the concepts learned in this session in a fun and engaging way.

Session Nine

# Growing Your Talents: Work with a Purpose

## Session Objectives

○ Understand the Church's perspective on the role of work in human life.

○ Recognize the importance of balancing work with faith and family.

○ Know yourself: Assess your talents, build on your strengths, and minimize your weaknesses.

○ Learn how to succeed at job hunting: resumes and job interviews.

○ Understand your paycheck.

## Key Terms

Employer              Employee              Resume

Interview             Salary                Tax Withholding

W-4                   Federal Income Taxes  State Income Taxes

FICA and Medicare Taxes  W-2

## Bible and Catechism References

Proverbs 6:6–11: "Go to the ant, O sluggard; consider her ways, and be wise. Without having any chief, officer or ruler, she prepares her food in summer, and gathers her sustenance in harvest. How long will you lie there, O sluggard? When will you arise from your sleep? A little sleep, a little slumber, a little folding of the hands to rest, and poverty will come upon you like a vagabond, and want like an armed man."

Colossians 3:23–24: "Whatever your task, work heartily, as serving the Lord and not men, knowing that from the Lord you will receive the inheritance as your reward; you are serving the Lord Christ."

2 Thessalonians 3:7–10: "For you yourselves know how you ought to imitate us; we were not idle when we were with you, we did not eat any one's bread without paying, but with toil and labor we worked night and day, that we might not burden any of you. It was not because we have not that right, but to give you in our conduct an example to

imitate. For even when we were with you, we gave you this command: If any one will not work, let him not eat."

Catechism 2427: "Human work proceeds directly from persons created in the image of God and called to prolong the work of creation by subduing the earth, both with and for one another. Hence work is a duty: 'If any one will not work, let him not eat.' Work honors the Creator's gifts and the talents received from him. It can also be redemptive."

Philippians 2:3–8: "Do nothing from selfishness or conceit, but in humility count others better than yourselves. Let each of you look not only to his own interests, but also to the interests of others. Have this mind among yourselves, which was in Christ Jesus, who, though he was in the form of God, did not count equality with God a thing to be grasped, but emptied himself, taking the form of a servant, being born in the likeness of men. And being found in human form he humbled himself, and became obedient unto death, even death on a cross."

Exodus 20:9–11: "Six days you shall labor, and do all your work; but the seventh day is a Sabbath to the Lord your God; in it you shall not do any work, you, or your son, or your daughter, your manservant, or your maidservant, or your cattle, or the sojourner who is within your gates; for in six days the Lord made heaven and earth, the sea, and all that is in them, and rested the seventh day; therefore the Lord blessed the Sabbath day and hallowed it."

Catechism 2184-2185: "Just as God 'rested on the seventh day from all his work which he had done,' human life has a rhythm of work and rest. The institution of the Lord's Day helps everyone enjoy adequate rest and leisure to cultivate their familial, cultural, social, and religious lives. On Sundays and other holy days of obligation, the faithful are to refrain from engaging in work or activities that hinder the worship owed to God, the joy proper to the Lord's Day, the performance of the works of mercy, and the appropriate relaxation of mind and body. Family needs or important social service can legitimately excuse from the obligation of Sunday rest. The faithful should see to it that legitimate excuses do not lead to habits prejudicial to religion, family life, and health."

## Reading

There is no getting around it: Work is going to be a big part of your life. If you work an average of forty hours per week for fifty years, you'll spend 104,000 hours at work. That's 6,240,000 minutes! The average amount of time a person spends in school from first grade through high school is about 20,000 hours. You may feel like you've been in school forever, but work will fill the equivalent of five high school educations! This fact can either depress or exhilarate you. It depends on your perspective toward work. You will, of course, want it to be rewarding on many levels: physically, spiritually, intellectually, and financially.

## Work with a Purpose: Responsibility and Gift

The references from Scripture and the Catechism noted at the beginning of the session convey a few important principles regarding work. As with the other subjects covered, if you get these key principles right, you can be confident that when you reach the later years of your life and reminisce, you'll have positive responses to the following questions:

𝕺 Did I use the natural talents the Lord gave me in ways that gave glory to him?

𝕺 Did I work hard at growing my God-given talents?

𝕺 Am I content with how I set my life's priorities, recognizing the substantial role that work plays, but keeping God and family as my highest priorities?

𝕺 Was I an effective team player, bringing out the best in those around me? Or, was I so focused on getting ahead that I ran over people in the process?

𝕺 Did I pursue work with passion?

Some think of work in a negative way, as something to be endured. This is quite natural for fallen human beings but also sad and unfortunate. Sure, there are times when work can be monotonous, but it is important to remember that it provides an opportunity to participate in God's creative and redemptive plan for mankind. Simply put, work has a purpose. And that purpose goes well beyond earning a living and providing for your family. It includes using your God-given talents to make a positive difference in this world.

Below is a letter I received from a gentleman who shared with me how his grandfather approached work. It captures the essence of what work is all about.

**Dear Phil,**

My grandfather was a dentist in Central Iowa in the 1930s. He was a committed dentist whose last resort was to pull a tooth.

Unfortunately, people who were struggling with basic needs did not practice the best dental hygiene. My grandfather was often called in "too late" and had to pull a molar out rather than fill a cavity—often in exchange for a chicken, a dozen eggs or a gallon of milk.

This led my grandfather to consider a teaching career, and he left the small town, moved to the University of Iowa in Iowa City in 1938 when my mother (an only child) was in 8th grade, and became a professor at the University of Iowa Dental College. He held his teaching position until 1972 when he retired after training a generation and a half of dentists to practice the "good dentistry" that was not possible during the Depression. He used his gift of teaching to spread good dental hygiene and practice.

When I was a boy, I was treated by one of my grandfather's former students, an orthodontist in Sioux City. After quite an extensive regime of treatment, my mother asked him "to send the bill and please to allow a little time to pay" as I was the oldest of seven and a large dental bill was the last thing my parents needed to pay. The orthodontist's response was, "You don't owe me anything. Without your father's training, I would not have had my profession. It is the least I can do to treat his grandson as a gift back."

This story is a great illustration of how one man effectively used the skills God had given him to better his own life and the lives of those around him. It is also a lesson in learning to give thanks to those who have mentored us along the way.

As you read and reflect on the Scripture and Catechism references at the beginning of this session, a few key themes emerge: the value of hard work, balance, and developing and using our talents well. Let's look at each of these.

## There Is Value in Hard Work . . .

Scripture and the Catechism make it clear that work is a duty (Proverbs 6:6–11; Colossians 3:23–24; 2 Thessalonians 3:7–10; Catechism 2427). In fact, Scripture says, "If any one will not work, let him not eat." (2 Thessalonians 3:10) Those are strong words—and of course they refer to able-bodied people. But make no mistake, we are expected to provide for ourselves and the common good.

Establish a strong work ethic early on. By following a few basics, you'll be a valued employee and be entrusted with increased responsibilities and financial rewards:

6 Be so reliable that your employer would trust you with his life. Integrity matters. Start work on time, apply yourself diligently to the work at hand, and be honest in all your dealings. With these attributes as your foundation, your employer will know he can depend on you.

○ Plan your work and work your plan. Follow through on commitments.

○ Be a team player. Don't let a competitive spirit lead to envy or jealousy with co-workers.

○ Never stop growing your talents and abilities. Participate in company-sponsored education programs if offered, or sign up for continuing education programs on your own. You need to stay current in your field of expertise so that you will always have the best there is to offer.

○ Go above and beyond the call of duty. Do more than is asked of you.

## . . . But Keep It in Balance

A strong work ethic is important, but even more important is learning how to set balanced priorities, including the priorities of faith and family.

The Lord has made it clear that we need to make our relationship with him a priority, and that takes time. We are to keep holy the Sabbath by resting and worshipping on the Lord's Day. (Ex. 20:9–11; CCC 2184–2185)

More and more, Sunday has become just the second day of the weekend. Businesses seek that extra dollar and calendars are filled with sports activities. Make an effort to have your Sundays be different from the rest of the week, with your day centered on participation at Mass and reception of the Holy Eucharist.

Also, make Sundays a special day for your family, and reserve time for rest so you can recharge your batteries.

## Know Yourself: Assess Your Talents, Build Your Strengths, Minimize Your Weaknesses

In a previous session, we discussed personality types, and you were encouraged to complete a personality profile. The understanding you gain from such a profile will give you keen insights into the types of careers that will make sense for you. If you especially like dealing with people, you want to make sure the work you seek takes that into account. If, on the other hand, you are a highly analytic person, it may be that a people-intensive career isn't what you would be drawn to or what would best

employ your talents. Of course, most careers require a blend of many talents. The point is to choose one that takes advantage of the natural gifts you have and allows you to blossom.

## Resumes and Employer Applications and Interviews

Most job offers are made at the end of what can be a long process for both the applicant and the potential employer. Employers make a big investment when they hire a new employee and they want to make sure they are making the right choice. It is just as important for applicants to have a good understanding of the organization they hope to work for and the role they would fill. That is why the hiring process is so involved. Depending on the job being sought, it can be a little like courtship!

Companies communicate the availability of positions in a variety of ways, including on their Web site, in advertisements, at job fairs, and of course, the old fashioned way: by word of mouth. While the level of information provided may be limited, make sure to take seriously the requirements they set for the position. Employers typically receive many responses to job advertisements from folks who clearly don't match the requirements of the position. Respect people's time and only apply for positions that offer a good fit.

You will probably be asked to submit a résumé, which is meant to provide a snapshot of why you are interested in the position and why you think you are qualified for it. A good résumé should be neat, organized, to the point, and show the following:

⚬ Career objective

⚬ Work experience

⚬ Education

⚬ Volunteer work

⚬ Hobbies and interests

You can find an example of a solid résumé in the Appendix.

The next step in the hiring process is normally the employer interview. Interviews for some positions are brief and involve only one person from the employer. Other positions may involve multiple interviewers and take place over several days. For a successful interview:

⚬ Be yourself.

⚬ Present yourself well.
  • Use a dress code equivalent to that used by the potential

employer, and maybe a step above.

- Take care of personal hygiene issues.

 Know your potential employer.
- Visit their Web site.
- Read articles about them in the news.

 Be a good listener.
- Answer questions forthrightly.

 Exhibit a genuine excitement over becoming part of your potential employer's team and help them understand how you can make their team better.

 Follow up with thank you notes to all interviewers no later than the day after the interview.

 Follow up by phone or e-mail as you deem appropriate. You want to show your interest while not becoming a bother. Respect the guidelines the potential employer gives for communication during the hiring process.

## Managing Your Paycheck

Once hired, your new employer will get you oriented to your new position. You'll be asked to complete certain paperwork, some of which is required by your employer and some of which is required by the government.

If you thought you'd receive your full salary, think again! For example, if you are paid biweekly and your annual salary is $48,000, you may expect your check to be for $1,846.15 ($48,000/26). Not so. There is a lovely little thing called tax withholding that you need to factor in.

One of the papers you'll be asked to complete is Form W-4, a federal form that will determine how much will be withheld from your paycheck for income tax. Taxes are withheld so you don't need to come up with one big payment when you file your annual tax return. A sample W-4 is included in the Appendix.

Not only will federal income taxes be withheld from your paycheck, but also state income taxes, FICA (Social Security) and Medicare taxes, as well as other state or local taxes depending on where you live. As a result, you'll actually receive a fair amount less than your agreed-upon salary. Depending on the job, additional amounts may be withheld for health insurance, retirement, or other items like tools and uniforms. The bottom line is that your check won't be for your "gross pay," but for the "net pay" after all the deductions are made.

A sample paycheck is included in the Appendix.

If your employer offers electronic direct deposit (your net pay is automatically deposited into your bank account), take advantage of it. You'll still receive a summary of that pay period's information. Use it to update your checkbook and budget.

Each year, by January 31, your employer is required to provide you with a summary of your earnings and taxes withheld on form W-2. You will use this information to complete your annual income tax returns. A sample form W-2 is included in the Appendix.

## Summary

Remember that work, though a duty, is also a gift from God that allows us to develop and use our talents in ways that benefit not only ourselves, but those around us as well.

## Discussion Topics

Read the discussion topic questions and write down your thoughts. This should be done prior to your class or small group get-together. In your class or small group, you'll share your thoughts with each other. For those discussion topics that list a Bible or Catechism reference, review it by referring to the applicable text at the beginning of the session.

## Discussion Topic 1
## Catechism 2427

Reread the reference noted above. Think about your career goals for the future. List at least five of them and describe how they correspond to the principles about work described in this reading.

_____

_____

_____

_____

_____

_____

_____

_____

_____

_____

## Discussion Topic 2

List at least five things you would do to prepare for an employer interview.

_____

_____

_____

_____

_____

_____

_____

_____

_____

_____

_____

## Activity

Follow the instructions of your teacher/leader as he (or she) guides you through this session's activity. The activity is designed to help you apply the concepts learned in this session in a fun and engaging way.

## Session Ten

# Being a Savvy Consumer

## Session Objectives

- Understand how best practices will help you be a smart spender.

- Understand credit scores and credit reports.

- Learn about how consumer finance protection laws affect you.

- Understand how to establish credit.

- Understand insurance basics.

- Recognize the risks associated with gambling.

## Key Terms

Credit Bureau

Credit Report

Credit Score

FICO Score

Fair Debt Collection Practices Act

Fair Credit Reporting Act

Truth in Lending Act

Deductible

Types of Insurance: Health, Auto, Renter's, Identity Theft Protection, Homeowner's, Disability, Life, Long-Term Care

## Bible and Catechism References

Proverbs 27:23: "Know well the condition of your flocks, and give attention to your herds."

Catechism 2410-2411: "Promises must be kept and contracts strictly observed to the extent that the commitments made in them are morally just. . . . Contracts are subject to commutative justice which regulates exchanges between persons and between institutions in accordance with a strict respect for their rights. Commutative justice obliges strictly; it requires safeguarding property rights, paying debts, and fulfilling obligations freely contracted."

Catechism 2413: "Games of chance (card games, etc.) or wagers are not in themselves contrary to justice. They become morally unacceptable when they deprive someone of what is necessary to provide for his needs and those of others. The passion for gambling risks becoming an enslavement. Unfair wagers and cheating at games constitute grave matter, unless the damage inflicted is so slight that the one who suffers it cannot reasonably consider it significant."

# Reading

The average household income in America is roughly $50,000. Obviously, there are wide variations; but the point is this: With limited resources, you need to be a savvy consumer if you want to succeed financially. You'll want to spend your money wisely, manage your credit profile well, and understand how to use insurance to limit financial risk.

## Best Practices for Being a Smart Spender

Savvy consumers understand that they can make their income stretch a whole lot further by being smart spenders. It's not rocket science, but it does take commitment and a few best practices.

The first best practice is pretty simple: Have a spending plan and stick to it. Is it as easy to put into practice as it is to state it? Let's just say this is a time when you can really prove your ability to delay gratification. When you go out to an "all you can eat" buffet, don't you find that your eyes are bigger than your stomach? The same is true with other types of consumption. There will always be that next thing you want, and you'll go broke if you spend on a whim. Set spending priorities in your budget (including fun money), then stick to the plan unless it's a life-or-death situation (or just about).

The second best practice is to become a comparison shopper. Whether you are buying a house, an automobile, insurance, or groceries, recognize that you have more than one option when it comes to making a purchase. The Internet is an invaluable tool for comparison shopping. When you need to make a large purchase or spend money on a recurring service, check at least three different sources before making a final decision. Of course, you want to buy products and services that are worth your money, so make sure you compare apples to apples. But even among reputable vendors, prices vary widely for equivalent products and services. It pays to do your homework.

A third best practice when it comes to spending is to avoid getting caught with brand-name merchandise for the wrong reason. Of course, there is value to a brand, which is why companies spend so much money promoting and protecting their image. When you purchase a particular brand because of the quality of the product, that's fine. But when you buy a product to gain prestige and admiration ("I'm going to look so good in that new jacket!"), you're setting yourself up for spiritual and financial disappointment.

A fourth best spending practice is to sleep on it when it comes to a big purchase. Whether it's a house, car, big screen TV, or investment, be careful about letting your emotions take control of the buying process. Sales people are taught how to close the sale, and they know if they get you to make the purchase emotionally, you are likely to follow with the real thing.

Finally, a great way to stretch your resources is to buy used when the circumstances make sense. Although you won't get the "wow" factor of buying something new, and you will need to complete due diligence to make sure you aren't getting a lemon, strategically buying used items—from houses, to cars, to clothing, and everything in-between—is being a savvy consumer. A whole industry has developed on the Internet to assist consumers with this. Take advantage of it.

## Credit Scores, Credit Reports and Consumer Protection Laws

Once you start using credit, your transaction data will be tracked by many organizations beyond just the business you owe. In order to provide lenders with the information they need to make good lending decisions, many businesses track and analyze credit information.

There are three primary credit bureaus that track your credit activity. These are Equifax, Experian, and TransUnion. Each of these makes your information available to lenders to assist them in making lending decisions. You are entitled to a free copy of your credit report from each of the three companies once a year (annualcreditreport.com), and you should take advantage of that. Make sure to review all information for accuracy, and if there is inaccurate data, contact the company (in writing) and ask them to correct your report. See a sample credit report in the Appendix.

Other companies have created scoring methods based on the data found in your credit report. The most well-known of these is Fair Isaac Corporation. They produce a credit score known as a FICO score, which lenders use to gauge your creditworthiness. Good credit management is key. Over your lifetime lower interest costs can save you tens if not hundreds of thousands of dollars.

Here is an example. Let's say you are planning to purchase a home and expect to borrow $250,000 in the form of a 30-year mortgage. Based on today's interest rates, assuming you had a top FICO score (760–850), the interest you pay over the 30-year period would amount to $213,000. However, if your score was in the range of 620–639, you would pay interest of $304,000. That's a difference of $91,000! The lender will force you to pay a higher interest rate because you are a higher risk.

FICO uses commonsense measures to determine your credit score. Payment history, amounts owed, the length of your credit history, and the addition of recent credit all factor in to your score. You can learn more at MyFICO.com.

## Consumer Protection Laws and You

In an effort to avoid abuses and to provide a certain level of consistency in the practices of lenders, the Federal government has, over the years, passed laws to regulate aspects of consumer lending.

Some of the better-known laws include:

- Fair Debt Collection Practices Act

- Fair Credit Reporting Act

- Truth in Lending Act

You can find more information at ftc.gov, but you don't need to become an expert on each of these laws. Just know that Congress requires certain standards of behavior from those in the financial industry, including:

- Limiting debt collection calls to between 8 a.m. and 9 p.m. local time.

- Prohibiting abusive language when communicating with a borrower regarding collection issues.

- Obliging credit reporting companies to provide one free credit report per year.

- Setting standards for correcting errors on credit reports.

- Setting standard financial disclosures about loan terms.

You can learn specifics at fdic.gov.

## Establishing Credit

For most young people (especially those in college), the challenge won't be establishing credit, but being patient enough not to rush the credit decision. We've already discussed how to manage debt and understand the difference between productive and unproductive debt. Although credit cards provide a convenient way to make day-to-day purchases, you should only have them in your financial toolbox if you use them for making purchases that are part of your spending plan and if you commit yourself to paying the bill in full every month. Otherwise, they will be harmful to your financial future. If you can't manage them well, rely on cash or your debit card.

With that said, many of you will make use of credit cards and that means you need to establish credit at some point. A good time to do so is while you are still in college, since finance companies view college students as good credit risks, primarily as a result of their future earnings potential. They also hope to establish a relationship with you early that will last a lifetime. There is typically no need to establish credit until the start of your career is in sight —even when tickets to see your favorite band go on sale. This is, however, a great time to exercise patience and wait until about six months prior to your graduation. You can do it, and you will love yourself for it later.

## Insurance Basics

If you are going to be a savvy consumer, you need to understand the true purpose of insurance. Insurance is a tool to help people manage financial risk in their lives. It is best thought of as a way to avoid "catastrophic" financial loss. Here are some examples when it is good to have insurance:

○ Your house burns down.

○ You cause a car accident, a victim is maimed for life, and they sue you to collect damages.

○ You develop a serious illness that requires hundreds of thousands of dollars in medical care.

Of course, such catastrophes only happen to a relatively small number of people. And that's the point when it comes to insurance. Large pools of people pay reasonably affordable premiums so that they can be protected in the event something bad happens to them. Because many people are paying in, and really bad things only happen to a few, the system works.

Many people make the mistake of wanting insurance to pay for minor bumps and bruises rather than for major losses. Purchasing insurance in this way is sure to bust most budgets. Instead, you should purchase insurance with relatively high deductibles and pay for minor losses out of your emergency and rainy day funds.

What types of insurance will you probably need during the course of your life? Here is a list you'll want to become familiar with (see descriptions in the Appendix):

- Health

- Auto

- Renters

- Identity theft

- Homeowners

- Life

- Disability

- Long-Term care

## A Word about Gambling

George Bernard Shaw once wrote, "In gambling, the many must lose in order that the few may win." The opportunity for many to lose has increased dramatically over the last two decades. It used to be that if you wanted to gamble, you had to travel to Las Vegas or Atlantic City. That's no longer the case. The National Gambling Impact Study Commission reported that during the decade ending in 1999, states with legalized gambling increased from just two to forty-eight, excluding only Utah and Hawaii. And now with gambling available via the Internet, it's easier than ever to become ensnared in an activity that can cause real harm to your future.

Is it wrong to gamble? Here is what the Church says about games of chance: "They become morally unacceptable when they deprive someone of what is necessary to provide for his needs and those of others. The passion for gambling risks becoming an enslavement." (CCC 2413) While it's clear that gambling is not inherently wrong, it does become a source of bondage for many. Here are a few statistics from Focus on the Family to consider (www.focusonthefamily. com/socialissues/gambling/ gambling/cause-for-concern.aspx):

- Within fifty miles of a casino, the prevalence of problem and pathological gamblers roughly doubles.

- SMR Research Corporation called gambling "the single fastest-growing driver of bankruptcy."

- The percentage of pathological gamblers among arrestees was three to five times higher than the general population, and compulsive or pathological gamblers were significantly more likely to have sold drugs than arrestees who fit the other gambling types.

- In the National Gambling Impact Study, the lifetime divorce rates for problem and pathological gamblers were 39.5 percent and 53.5 percent, respectively; the rate in non-gamblers was 18.2 percent.

- Three years after casinos were legalized in Deadwood, South Dakota, felony crimes increased by 40 percent, child abuse increased 42 percent, and domestic violence and assaults rose 80 percent.

It is clear that compulsive gambling leads to serious

personal and financial problems. While most people who gamble don't fall into the compulsive or pathological categories, it's important that you know and be honest with yourself when it comes to setting boundaries for gambling.

It is one thing to read about statistics, another to think about the real lives underneath those facts. Let me share a true story with you. After getting married to Sue and starting a family, Ed became restless and looked to gambling as a source of excitement. What started as a "once in a while" activity during his lunch break became an addiction that led to lying to his wife, amassing debts of $140,000 on twenty-eight different credit cards, even embezzling from his employer.

As the pressure of growing debts and a false life increased, it all became an overwhelming burden for Ed, who even pondered suicide. Thankfully, he eventually sought help, and came clean with Sue and with his employer. However, his actions had consequences. Ed was convicted of embezzlement and spent a brief time in prison. He and Sue had to declare bankruptcy. You can imagine how, from Sue's perspective, it would have been easy to pack her bags and leave. But, with God's grace, she remained committed to Ed and their marriage. It's a testimony to the power of forgiveness and redemption that over months and years they overcame Ed's gambling problems. But wouldn't it have been better had he avoided gambling in the first place? Dear young people, I encourage you to stay far away from the dangers associated with compulsive gambling and instead seek more wholesome forms of entertainment.

## Summary

By applying consumer best practices, using credit cards wisely, understanding your credit report and credit score, and avoiding compulsive gambling, you'll be a savvy consumer and be able to stretch your resources to meet your financial goals.

## Discussion Topics

Read the discussion topic questions and write down your thoughts. This should be done prior to your class or small group get-together. In your class or small group, you'll share your thoughts with each other. For those discussion topics that list a Bible or Catechism reference, review it by referring to the applicable text at the beginning of the session.

# Discussion Topic 1

Describe five best practices for being a savvy consumer and give examples of how each can apply in a real-life circumstance.

_____

_____

_____

_____

_____

_____

_____

_____

_____

_____

## Discussion Topic 2
## Catechism 2413

If someone takes part in gambling, how can he tell whether he is enjoying it as a reasonable form of recreation as opposed to it "becoming an enslavement" as the Catechism describes?

_____

_____

_____

_____

_____

_____

_____

_____

_____

# Activity

Follow the instructions of your teacher/leader as he (or she) guides you through this session's activity. The activity is designed to help you apply the concepts learned in this session in a fun and engaging way.

Session Eleven

# Getting Started in Real Estate

## Session Objectives

- ⊙ Understand the basics of renting.

- ⊙ Learn how to purchase your first house.

- ⊙ Understand home loans.

- ⊙ Learn how to sell your home successfully.

- ⊙ Understand the basics of real estate investing.

## Key Terms

| | |
|---|---|
| Tenant | Landlord |
| Real Estate Broker/Agent | Mortgage |
| Interest-Only Loan | Graduated Payment Loan |
| Negative Amortization Loan | Balloon Payment Loan |
| Adjustable-Rate Loan | Fixed-Rate Loan |
| Principal | Down Payment |
| Private Mortgage Insurance | Conventional Loan |
| FHA Loan | VA Loan |
| Interest Rate | Annual Percentage Rate (APR) |
| Loan Origination Fees | Points |
| Lock-In Agreement | Appraisal |
| Title | Title Insurance |
| Escrow | Equity |
| Transaction, Settlement, or Closing Costs | |

## Bible and Catechism References

Proverbs 24:27: "Prepare your work outside, get everything ready for you in the field; and after that build your house."

Proverbs 27:23: "Know well the condition of your flocks, and give attention to your herds."

Luke 14:28–29: "For which of you, desiring to build a tower, does not first sit down and count the cost, whether he has enough to complete it? Otherwise, when he has laid a foundation, and is not able to finish, all who see it begin to mock him, saying, 'This man began to build, and was not able to finish.'"

## Reading

Real estate is for everyone. From renting, to owning your own home, even investing in real estate where others live or work, real estate has something to offer everyone. However, it is important that you become educated about real estate before you get involved with it. Of course, this is just an introduction, but by learning the principles discussed here, you'll be equipped to make wise real estate decisions.

## The Basics of Renting

There's a common saying, "Why waste money on renting when you can own instead?" While there is a great deal of truth in that statement, there are many situations in which it makes sense to rent. Scripture speaks of taking time to get our affairs in order before making a big commitment to property: "Prepare your work outside, get everything ready for you in the field; and after that build your house." (Proverbs 24:27)

Unless you expect to own a property for a substantial period of time—five to seven years is a good minimum—it is better to rent than to buy. Why? Because buying and selling property is expensive. Assuming you're financing the purchase—getting a mortgage, that is—you'll incur closing costs that can easily total 2% of the loan amount. That's $4,000 on a $200,000 loan. When you sell the property, you'll have to pay the real estate agent's fee, the cost of sprucing up the property to make it attractive to a buyer, a homeowner's warranty policy, and other expenses. These can easily come to 8% or more of the sales price. When you include expenses related to the purchase and the sale, it means that a property needs to sell for 10% more than you originally paid just to break even.

Real estate investors expect to recover these costs through a combination of positive cash flow from renting the property and price appreciation, which occurs over time. Homeowners depend solely on price appreciation. In the long run, property values historically increase at about the rate of inflation. As a result, you can expect it to take several years to recover the transaction costs related to property ownership.

Another situation in which it makes sense to rent is when you are new to an area. Buying property is a big deal, and you should thoroughly understand the local real estate market before making such a commitment. You'll want to ask yourself these questions: What are you looking for in a property? Do you want a country or urban lifestyle? How close do you want to be to work and your children's schools? Can you afford the areas you find desirable? Renting provides an opportunity to get to know an area well before buying.

Another reason to bide your time is that real estate activity is cyclical. If you are in the market for property during a cyclical bubble, it may make sense to wait for the bubble to burst and for prices to soften. You may find that you can save tens of thousands of dollars by being patient.

## Renting Your First Place

Before you rent your first place you'll want to answer a few questions:

○ How much does it make sense to spend?

○ How will you find the right place?

○ Do you need insurance as a renter?

Before you start looking for an apartment or room to rent, it is important to determine how much you can afford to spend. The best way to do this is to prepare an annual budget with the expenses you expect to incur when you start renting. Depending on your lease, in addition to basic rent, you may also incur additional charges for common facilities such as washing machines, dryers, and utilities. Upon signing as a tenant, you may also have to provide the landlord with first and last month's rent as well as a security deposit and proof of renter's insurance. You'll want to understand these charges and have sufficient cash in the bank to cover them before you sign any agreement. Make sure the ongoing expenses fit into your overall budget and that they allow you to meet your other obligations.

Once you know how much you expect to spend, you can begin your search. Make a list of the most important attributes you are looking for, including:

○ Location, including general desirability and proximity to work, school, family, and other places of interest to you.

○ Size, including number of bedrooms, once you've determined whether you are planning on sharing with a roommate.

○ Amenities, such as pool, exercise facilities, clubhouse, and parking.

○ Acceptance of pets, if you have any.

○ If multi-story, do you prefer the ground or top floor? Remember that if you choose the ground floor, you can expect noise from the room above you.

With your budget information and list of attributes, you are in a position to begin your search. Asking family, friends, and co-workers for places that match your criteria is a great way to start. If you have acquaintances who are real estate brokers or agents, they will be happy to share their knowledge. Make sure to treat them to something nice for doing so. You can formally contract with a realtor to find a place for you and assist you with the rental agreement process, but expect to pay them a fee equivalent to a month's rent. Having a relationship established with a realtor well before you consider purchasing a house will be a big plus.

## Buying Your First House

While the time a person rents will vary based on circumstances, in most cases, it will eventually make sense to purchase a home. Just as with renting, you need to determine how much you can afford, the area in which you want to live, and the basic attributes you are looking for in your home. However, you'll want to be confident in the structural soundness of the home, understand your financing options, and know how to negotiate with the seller, which will include establishing a relationship with a realtor. Let's go through these one at a time.

One of the most common mistakes people make when purchasing a home is buying more than they can afford. It is an exciting time, and it's easy to get caught up in that excitement. People often depend on their lender to tell them how large a mortgage they qualify for. Remember, lenders make money by loaning money. The system largely rewards them for the volume of lending they do, rather than on doing what's good for you. Instead of letting the lender tell you how much house you can buy, you'll be far better off telling the lender how much you can afford. You do that by updating your existing budget, and creating a financial forecast that includes the estimated costs of home ownership.

I find it works well when all housing-related expenses, including payment, property taxes, insurance, maintenance, utilities, landscaping, and improvements are between 30% and 35% of gross income. When you spend beyond this, it will be difficult to fund other important areas, including saving, education, and insurance.

## Looking for the Right Home—Location, Location, Location!

Once you know how much house you can afford, the next step is to determine the main attributes you want in your home. There is a saying in real estate: "Location, location, location!" After affordability, there is no more important factor when buying your home than location. After all, what good is it to find just the house you want if you don't feel safe when you go outside, or, if noise from a freeway, railroad, or other source will be a daily nuisance?

What attributes do you want in your home? Rural or urban? Attached or single-family? Big yard or small? How many bedrooms? One story or two? How many square feet? Share these thoughts with family and friends who live in the area and ask them to suggest neighborhoods that fit your description.

## Establishing a Relationship with a Realtor

By this time, you'll need to have established a relationship with a realtor. A good realtor will be extremely knowledgeable about your local housing market and will be your advocate during negotiations with the seller.

Realtors can represent the buyer, seller, or both. You should find a realtor who only represents your interests. It is easy to see how it could be difficult for a realtor to be objective when representing both buyer and seller.

## Financing the Purchase of Your House

Before you can effectively comparison shop for a mortgage, you need to make important decisions regarding the type of borrowing you want to do. Back when my parents were getting a mortgage, things were pretty simple. They made a 20% down payment, got a loan for the remaining 80% of the purchase price, and made a fixed payment for 30 years. There weren't any surprises.

In an effort to make housing more affordable, "creative" loan products were developed that reduced the amount of money buyers needed to get into a home. Down payments were reduced, sometimes to zero. Monthly payments were also reduced so that only the interest on the loan (if that) had to be paid in the short run. This has the effect of kicking obligations down the road and leads to serious financial consequences. These creative loans include interest-only, graduated payment, negative amortization, balloon payment, and many adjustable rate loans. I recommend you stay away from all of them.

Instead of getting a mortgage full of surprises, I recommend you choose a home loan that fits the following criteria:

○ Provides a fixed rate and payment over the life of the loan.

○ Pays down the loan's principal balance in a straightforward manner (i.e., no balloon payments or negative amortization).

○ Has a repayment period that is linked to when your oldest child enters college. The challenge of paying for college will be lightened by being mortgage free!

## A Word on Down Payments

As noted above, much has changed with mortgages over the years, including the level of down payment required. When 20% down payments were the norm, it meant that everyone had skin in the game. That, in turn, led to stability in housing prices. As the requirements for down payments and other mortgage terms were eased, house prices became more volatile.

During the early 2000s, housing prices increased dramatically, often at an annual rate of 20% or more, for several years. This was unsustainable, and in 2008, we experienced a major financial and housing crisis. Prices declined by 50% or more in some places. Buyers who made 20% down payments just prior to the downturn lost their down payment (at least in the short run).

That raises the question of whether it is smart to make a 20% down payment or not. While I wish that lenders would require 20% down payments so that house prices would tend to be more stable, until they do, you may want to consider making the lowest down payment required by the lender. With that said, because purchasing a house is a substantial long-term commitment, I recommend that you have the equivalent of a 20% down payment saved before you purchase a home. Use the minimum amount required for the down payment and keep the remainder as part of your general rainy day fund.

Note that when less than a 20% down payment is made, lenders will require private mortgage insurance as additional security that the loan will be repaid. The cost of such insurance will add about $700 per year to the cost of your mortgage for every $100,000 financed.

## Mortgage Shopping

Just as with other major purchases, it makes sense to shop around for the best mortgage deal you can find. Mortgages are available from many sources, including commercial banks, credit unions, and mortgage companies. You can also hire a mortgage broker who acts as a middleman between you and those institutions and holds your hand through the process. Use the Mortgage Shopping Worksheet in the appendix as a template for your comparison shopping. By doing so, you'll likely save tens of thousands of dollars over the life of your loan.

## Choosing a Shorter Mortgage Term and Prepaying a Mortgage: The Pros and Cons

One of the decisions you'll need to make when looking at loan alternatives is the term of the loan—how long you'll take to pay the loan off. Thirty-year mortgages used to be the norm, but there is a greater variety today. Of course, the longer the term, the lower your monthly payment. While that may be enticing, it's also true that the longer the term the longer you'll be in debt and the more interest you'll pay. I prefer a path that builds equity more quickly and allows you to be mortgage free by the time your oldest child enters college. What are the benefits of paying your mortgage off faster than the typical thirty years?

○ You'll save lots of interest (see Exhibit 1 below).

○ Your cash flow will be increased dramatically when your mortgage is paid off.

○ Your ability to fund college for your children will be enhanced.

○ The burden of owing money to someone else will be lifted.

There is an opportunity cost to paying off your mortgage in a shorter time frame. The money you spend on it can't be used in other ways, whether it's for investing or day-to-day spending. A reasonable argument against a shorter-term mortgage or making prepayments on a mortgage is that it is possible to invest those funds and obtain a rate of return greater than the mortgage interest you are paying. If you did that, you'd come out ahead, financially speaking. Of course, there is no guarantee that you would invest the difference. The reality is that a lot of people spend it. And although long-term investments in many cases should provide a higher rate of return than the interest on your mortgage, there's no guarantee. Given the peace of mind that comes with being debt free, prepaying your mortgage makes sense.

Here is one example of the interest savings generated by paying a mortgage in fifteen years rather than thirty years:

Here is another important point to consider. Just because you choose to pay down your mortgage early doesn't mean you shouldn't be contributing to retirement and college savings plans at the same time. Remember the importance of compounding earnings on the ability to create wealth. You need to build all these requirements into your cash flow plan.

# Exhibit 1: The Effect of Prepaying a Mortgage

|  | 30-Year Loan | 15-Year Loan |
|---|---|---|
| **Original Loan Amount** | $200,000 | $200,000 |
| **Interest Rate** | 6.0% | 5.5% |
| **Monthly Payment** | $1,199.10 | $1,634.17 |
| **Difference in Monthly Payments** | N/A | $435.07 |
| **Total Cash Paid During Term of Loan** | $431,676.00 | $294,150.60 |
| **Interest Saved** | N/A | $137,525.40 |

## Real Estate as an Investment

Many people limit their real estate activity to their home and indirect investments such as real estate stocks and mutual funds. Others recognize that real estate provides an opportunity to create wealth, and choose to become part-time or full-time real estate investors.

Too often, inexperienced real estate investors jump in hoping to make fast money, and frequently pay a heavy price. The wealth effect of real estate occurs over a long period of time. Wise investors recognize this. Let me share two true stories.

The first involves a couple in their thirties who got interested in real estate, initially as a second source of income. Over the years, they had built up a reasonable amount of equity in their home. They attended a seminar on how to create wealth as a real estate investor. The instructor taught a strategy that encouraged borrowing against the equity in their home and using those funds as down payments (making as small a down payment as possible and borrowing the rest) on as many investment properties as the funds would allow.

At first, the strategy worked as prices continued to increase (this occurred during a major real estate bubble). Because of their early success, they doubled down, borrowing more against the equity of their personal residence so they could purchase additional rental properties. They even gave up their other work and focused on full-time investing. Eventually, the real estate bubble burst and prices declined by as much as 50%, with dire consequences. Because they had spread their equity so thin across several properties, all their equity was lost when prices declined. They were forced to start their financial lives over, and now had ten fewer years to create the wealth they would need to fund their retirement and other financial goals.

Contrast the experience of this couple with friends of my parents. This couple purchased a duplex as their first property. They lived in one of the apartments and rented out the other. Eventually, the rental income from the tenant was sufficient to cover the total mortgage payment, so in essence they had "free" housing. That freed up enough funds for them to add another property, and so on. The expertise they developed in the local real estate market attracted funding from additional investors, which allowed them to multiply their efforts further.

While this couple also used debt to finance their properties, they limited their borrowing to prudent levels, and were disciplined in managing the cash flow of their properties. They didn't grow their investments as rapidly as the first couple in the early years, but their steady hand led to the creation of extensive wealth.

Why did one couple lose all they had while the other couple successfully created wealth? The answer boils down to understanding debt and managing investments for the long term. The first couple got caught up in the frenzy of a housing bubble and allowed themselves to become overly leveraged. The second couple showed patience, recognized the long-term nature of their investments, and limited their debt to sustainable levels.

Before you make a decision to become an active investor in real estate, assess your talents and the demands on your time so you can be confident that it makes sense for you. If you decide you want to take the next step, develop relationships with mentors who will share their experiences. Investors, realtors, bankers, contractors, and real estate attorneys all have valuable insights that will help you create a strategy for success.

## Summary

As I mentioned at the beginning, real estate is for everyone. The degree of your involvement in real estate will depend on personal circumstances and plans. By applying the principles and practices explained in this session, you'll be in a position to make real estate decisions that will serve you well for a lifetime.

## Discussion Topics

Read the discussion topic questions and write down your thoughts. This should be done prior to your class or small group get-together. In your class or small group, you'll share your thoughts with each other. For those discussion topics that list a Bible or Catechism reference, review it by referring to the applicable text at the beginning of the session.

## Discussion Topic 1
## Proverbs 24:27, Luke 14:28–29

Re-read the references noted above. Consider how you will know you are ready to purchase real estate. List the five most significant points you can think of and make sure to include non-financial as well as financial issues.

_____

_____

_____

_____

_____

_____

_____

_____

_____

_____

## Discussion Topic 2

Describe the pros and cons of choosing to pay a mortgage off in a shorter time frame than the standard thirty years.

_____

_____

_____

_____

_____

_____

_____

_____

_____

_____

## Activity

Follow the instructions of your teacher/leader as he (or she) guides you through this session's activity. The activity is designed to help you apply the concepts learned in this session in a fun and engaging way.

# Appendix

## Key Terms

(Definitions are from the Merriam-Webster online dictionary unless otherwise noted.)

## Session One

Principle:
- a comprehensive and fundamental law, doctrine, or assumption.
- a rule or code of conduct.
- habitual devotion to right principles.
- a primary source.

Value:
- something (as a principle or quality) intrinsically valuable or desirable.

Attitude:
- a mental position with regard to a fact or state.
- a feeling or emotion toward a fact or state.

Action:
- the accomplishment of a thing usually over a period of time, in stages, or with the possibility of repetition.

Bible:

- the sacred scriptures of Christians comprising the Old Testament and the New Testament.

*Catechism of the Catholic Church:*

- a summary of religious doctrine often in the form of questions and answers.

Financial Literacy:

- having knowledge or competence (in financial matters).

## Session Two

Bartering:

- trading by exchanging one commodity for another.

Currency:

- something (as coins, Treasury notes, and banknotes) that is in circulation as a medium of exchange.

Inflation:

- a continuing rise in the general price level usually attributed to an increase in the volume of money and credit relative to available goods and services.

Deflation:

- a contraction in the volume of available money or credit that results in a general decline in prices.

Hyperinflation:

- inflation growing at a very high rate in a very short time.

Federal Reserve System:

- the central banking system of the United States consisting of 12 districts with a Federal Reserve Bank in the principal commercial city of each district.

Gross Domestic Product:
- the gross national product excluding the value of net income earned abroad.

Taxes:
- a charge usually of money imposed by authority on persons or property for public purposes.

Liquidity:
- consisting of or capable of ready conversion into cash.
- capable of covering current liabilities quickly with current assets.

Recession:
- a period of reduced economic activity.

Depression:
- a period of low general economic activity marked especially by rising levels of unemployment.

Unemployment Rate:
- the state of being unemployed; involuntary idleness of workers; also the rate of such unemployment.

Socialization:
- to participate actively in a social group.

Subsidiarity:
- a principle in social organization: functions which subordinate or local organizations perform effectively belong more properly to them than to a dominant central organization.

*Rerum Novarum*: On the Condition of the Working Classes:
- an encyclical issued by Pope Leo XIII on May 15, 1891. It discussed the relationships and mutual duties between labor and obtaining capital, as well

as government and its citizens. It supported the rights of labor to form unions, rejected communism and unrestricted capitalism, while affirming the right to private property. (Wikipedia)

*Centesimus Annus*: On the Hundredth Anniversary of Rerum Novarum:

- an encyclical written by Pope John Paul II in 1991, on the hundredth anniversary of *Rerum Novarum*. It is part of a larger body of writings known as Catholic social teaching, that trace their origin to *Rerum Novarum*, which was issued by Pope Leo XIII in 1891, and ultimately the New Testament. (Wikipedia)

*Caritas in Veritate*: Charity in Truth:

- the third encyclical of Pope Benedict XVI and his first social encyclical. It was signed on June 29, 2009. The encyclical is concerned with the problems of global development and progress towards the common good of all peoples, arguing that both Love and Truth are essential elements of an effective response. (Wikipedia)

## Session Three

Creator:

- one that creates usually by bringing something new or original into being: God.

Owner:

- to have or hold as property, possess.

Manager:

- a person who conducts business or household affairs.

Steward of Providence:

- A person who uses the gifts and resources entrusted to him in ways pleasing to God. (Phil Lenahan)

Holiness (call to holiness, sanctification):

- the state of growing in divine grace as a result of Christian commitment after baptism or conversion.

Virtues:

- conformity to a standard of right, morality.

Vices:

- moral depravity or corruption.
- a moral fault or failing.

Capital Sins:

- Seven sins of pride, covetousness, lust, anger, gluttony, envy, and sloth held to be fatal to spiritual progress.

Spiritual Plan:

- Every method of examination of conscience, of meditation, of contemplation, of vocal and mental prayer, and of other spiritual activities [employed for the purpose] of seeking and finding the will of God in the disposition of our life for the salvation of our soul. (The Spiritual Exercises of St. Ignatius)

# The Virtues and Vices: Which Ones Describe You?

## Virtues

Virtue is a habitual and firm disposition to do what is good. The virtues are traditionally divided into two main groups, human and theological.*

The human virtues are stable states of the mind and the will that guide our actions and order our desires according to reason and faith. They can be grouped around the four cardinal virtues: prudence, justice, fortitude, and temperance.

Prudence helps us to figure out, in every circumstance, what is really good for us and to choose the right means for achieving it.

Justice consists in the firm and constant will to give God and neighbor their due.

Fortitude ensures strength in difficulties and endurance in seeking what is good.

Temperance helps us to be moderate and balanced in our appetites and our use of the goods given to us by God.

The theological virtues concern God directly. They are not ordered toward a balance between extremes, as the human virtues are. In other words, you can never have enough faith, hope, and love.

By faith, we believe in God and believe all that he has revealed to us and that the Church proposes for our belief. By hope, we desire eternal life as our happiness and trust God to grant us the graces needed to attain it.

By charity, we love God above all things and our neighbor as ourselves for love of God. Charity, the form of all the virtues, "binds everything together in perfect harmony" (Col. 3:14). (Kindness belongs under charity.)

The Holy Spirit brings seven gifts to Christians: wisdom, understanding, counsel, fortitude, knowledge, piety, and fear of the Lord.

## Vices

Vices are immoral or bad habits that pull us toward our weakness as fallen human beings and away from living according to our true dignity. The seven main categories of the vices (also known as the Seven Deadly Sins) are:

**Pride:** The root of all vice. Through pride, a person desires to be better than everyone else, and fails to acknowledge his proper place before God.

Pride is a doozie. It is the worst of the vices in the sense that it tears you away from your basic position before God as a creature in need of help. Without that grounding in reality, you'll decide you can do whatever you want, and the other vices follow along like baby ducks waddling after their mama.

**Envy:** To envy is to desire unhappily what someone else has. The envious person resents others for having good things that they feel they don't have, and is ungrateful for the good things God has given them.

Envy is a monster that eats up the life in a person. By fixating on how much more popular, smart, rich, or even virtuous another is, you destroy your ability to see yourself as a unique and unrepeatable being, loved with a love beyond your understanding.

**Gluttony**: Excessive concern with food or other goods. The gluttonous person might eat either too much, too soon, too eagerly, too daintily, and may even just think too much about food.

Who doesn't pop one too many M&M's once in a while? Or salivate over a juicy steak? Caring a lot about food is a totally human thing, and we're meant to enjoy it, but not so much that we're living to eat instead of eating to live. Food is fuel meant to enable us to lead lives of exuberance and energy, pressing toward the life to come; not to pull us away from our higher calling.

**Lust**: Sexual desire that is not put in its proper place and aimed at the whole person. The lustful person reduces another person to a mere physical object.

The human body makes us able to give and receive love in a physical way. A person has a dignity beyond the physical aspect, which his physical aspect expresses. That means that if you treat others as if they are just objects of physical desire, you're violating the truth about them and about yourself as human persons.

**Anger**: Uncontrolled resentment and indignation at a real or perceived offense. The angry person often seeks revenge for the things they have suffered.

Even when not shouting uncontrollably, a human being can have uncontrollable resentment boiling away in his chest. People are often angry without knowing it, feeling that something unfair was done to them; and then it might come out not as anger but as sadness or a closed-off attitude toward people. We're good at getting even, in small ways, with the people who have hurt us—by putting them down, using something the other person owns without asking, or talking about them behind their back.

**Greed**: Like gluttony, greed is over-concern for created goods, but particularly for money.

Scrooge was the worst kind of greedy person, because he didn't even want money for the sake of enjoying good things, like a beautiful home or a rare work of art. He just wanted to know that piles and piles of coins were his and no one else's.

**Sloth**: Laziness, indifference, unwillingness to act. The slothful person shirks duties and always takes the easy way out.

Most of us can see some sloth in us when that exam paper is due, or when the alarm clock buzzes at 6 a.m.

The seven virtues that are specific opposites of these seven vices are: humility against pride, kindness against envy, abstinence against gluttony, chastity against lust, patience against anger, generosity against greed, and diligence against sloth. (These are also numbered among the twelve fruits of the Holy Spirit.)

*See the *Catechism of the Catholic Church*, Article 7 (sections 1803–1845), for more about the virtues and vices.

## Session Four

Balance Sheet:
- a statement of financial condition at a given date.

Asset:
- an item of value owned.
- the items on a balance sheet showing the book value of property owned.

Liability:
- something for which one is liable; especially a pecuniary obligation debt.

Net Worth:
- the difference between assets and liabilities. (Phil Lenahan)

Budget:
- a statement of the financial position of an administration for a definite period of time based on estimates of expenditures during the period and proposals for financing them.
- a plan for the coordination of resources and expenditures.
- the amount of money that is available for, required for, or assigned to a particular purpose.

Income:
- a gain or recurrent benefit usually measured in money that derives from capital or labor; the amount of such gain received in a period of time

Expense:
- something expended to secure a benefit or bring about a result.
- financial burden or outlay; cost.
- an item of business outlay chargeable against revenue for a specific period.

Not Sufficient Funds (NSF):

- when an attempted bank withdrawal exceeds cash available in the account. (Phil Lenahan)

Bank Reconciliation:

- a periodic process (typically monthly) that insures bank activity and register activity maintained by the account holder are in agreement. (Phil Lenahan)

## Session Five

Detachment:

- Not to become overly attached to material things. (Phil Lenahan).

Compound Interest:

- Interest computed on the sum of an original principal and accrued interest.

Interest:

- The profit in goods or money that is made on invested capital.

Capital Gain:

- The increase in value of an asset (as stock or real estate) between the time it is bought and the time it is sold.

Rate of Return:

- The ratio of money gained or lost (whether realized or unrealized) on an investment relative to the amount of money invested. (Wikipedia)

Rule of 72:

- A method for estimating an investment's doubling time. (Wikipedia)

Risk/Return Relationship:

- A general rule in investing that as the rate of return increases, the risk required to generate the higher return also increases. (Phil Lenahan)

Tax-Free and Tax-Favored Investments:

- Investments that are either not subject to taxes (tax-free) or are otherwise given special tax treatment. (Phil Lenahan)

Reserve Funds: Emergency, Rainy Day, Retirement, College:

- Funds reserved for specific future uses. (Phil Lenahan)

Money Market Fund:

- The trade in short-term negotiable instruments (as certificates of deposit or Treasury securities).

Certificate of Deposit:

- A money market bond of a preset face value paying fixed interest and redeemable without penalty only on maturity.

Diversification:

- To balance (as an investment portfolio) defensively by dividing funds among securities of different industries or of different classes.

Asset Allocation:

- The strategy used in choosing in what asset classes such as stocks and bonds one wants to invest, given a person's appetite for and ability to shoulder risk. (Wikipedia)

Stock:

- The proprietorship (ownership) element in a corporation usually divided into shares and represented by transferable certificates.

Bond:
- An interest-bearing certificate of public or private indebtedness.

Commodities:
- An economic good: a product of agriculture or mining.

Mutual Fund:
- An open-end investment company that invests money of its shareholders in a usually diversified group of securities of other corporations.

Rebalancing:
- The action of bringing a portfolio of investments that has deviated away from one's target asset allocation back into line. Under-weighted securities can be purchased with newly saved money; alternatively, over-weighted securities can be sold to purchase under-weighted securities. (Wikipedia)

## Session Six

Productive Debt:
- Debt used prudently to purchase an appreciating and/or income-producing asset. (Phil Lenahan)

Unproductive Debt:
- Debt used to purchase depreciating assets or used imprudently or excessively to purchase appreciating and/or income producing assets. (Phil Lenahan)

Appreciating Asset:
- An asset that increases in value over time. (Phil Lenahan)

Income-Producing Asset:
- An asset that provides a regular income stream over time. (Phil Lenahan)

Depreciating Asset:
- An asset that decreases in value over time. (Phil Lenahan).

Amortization:
- A schedule reflecting the timing of debt repayment through regular payments of principal and interest. (Phil Lenahan)

Annual Percentage Rate:
- The effective annual interest rate on a loan, including fees that are added to the loan. (Phil Lenahan)

Minimum Payment:
- The minimum monthly payment required by the finance company. (Phil Lenahan)

Debit Card:
- An electronic payment option in which the amount of the purchase is taken out of one's bank account at the point of purchase. (Phil Lenahan)

Credit Card:
- An electronic payment option in which the card issuer (the finance company) provides payment to the vendor at the point of purchase and bills the cardholder for total purchases on a monthly basis. If payment is not made in a timely manner, substantial finance charges are incurred. (Phil Lenahan)

Accelerator Repayment Plan:
- A methodical approach to paying down unproductive debt in an accelerated manner in order to reduce interest expense paid and to become free of unproductive debt. (Phil Lenahan)

## Session Seven

Marriage (Matrimony):
- "The matrimonial covenant, by which a man and a woman establish between themselves a

partnership of the whole of life, is by its nature ordered toward the good of the spouses and the procreation and education of offspring; this covenant between baptized persons has been raised by Christ the Lord to the dignity of a sacrament." (CCC 1601)

Unity:
- oneness; state of being one or undivided; united in mind or purpose. (Wiktionary)

Honesty:
- To be truthful. (Wiktionary)

Counsel:
- The exchange of opinions and advice; consultation. (Wiktionary)

Talent:
- A marked natural ability or skill. (Wiktionary)

Family Budget Meeting:
- A periodic meeting including husband and wife (and children as appropriate) to review and discuss their financial status and plans. (Phil Lenahan)

Pre-existing Debt:
- Debt that an individual brings into a marriage. (Phil Lenahan)

Combined Financial Plan:
- A financial plan that combines assets, liabilities, income, and expenses for purposes of establishing family financial goals. (Phil Lenahan)

Joint Checking Account:
- A checking account that includes both husband and wife as authorized signers. (Phil Lenahan)

## Session Eight

Tithing:
- To pay or give a tenth part of income especially for the support of the church.

Legalistic:
- Strict, literal, or excessive conformity to the law or to a religious or moral code.

Scrupulous:
- Acting in strict regard for what is considered right or proper.

First Fruits:
- The earliest gathered fruits offered to the Deity in acknowledgment of the gift of fruitfulness.
- The earliest products or results of an endeavor.

## Session Nine

Employer:
- An individual or organization that provides a job that pays wages or a salary.

Employee:
- One employed by another usually for wages or salary.

Resume:
- A curriculum vitae or short account of one's career and qualifications prepared typically by an applicant for a position.

Interview:
- A formal consultation usually to evaluate qualifications (as of a prospective student or employee).

Salary:
- Fixed compensation paid regularly for services.

Tax Withholding:

- A deduction (as from wages, fees, or dividends) levied at the source of income as advance payment on income tax.

W-4:

- A tax form used by the Internal Revenue Service and employers to determine the correct amount of tax withholding to deduct from employees' wages. (Wikipedia)

Federal Income Taxes:

- The federal government of the United States imposes a progressive tax on the taxable income of individuals, partnerships, companies, corporations, trusts, decedents' estates, and certain bankruptcy estates. The first Federal income tax was imposed (under Article I, section 8, clause 1 of the U.S. Constitution) during the Civil War, then again in the 1890s, and again after the Sixteenth Amendment was ratified in 1913. (Wikipedia)

State Income Taxes

- An income tax levied by each individual state. (Wikipedia)

FICA and Medicare taxes:

- The Federal Insurance Contributions Act (FICA) tax is a payroll (or employment) tax imposed by the federal government on both employees and employers to fund Social Security and Medicare—federal programs that provide benefits for retirees, the disabled, and children of deceased workers. Social Security benefits include old-age, survivor's, and disability insurance. Medicare provides hospital insurance benefits. (Wikipedia)

W-2:

- Form W-2, Wage and Tax Statement, is used to report wages paid to employees and the taxes withheld from them. Relevant amounts on Form W-2 are reported by the Social Security Administration to the Internal Revenue Service. The form is also used to report FICA taxes to the Social Security Administration. Employers must complete a Form W-2 for each employee to whom they pay a salary, wage, or other compensation as part of the employment relationship. An employer must deliver the Form W-2 to employees on or before January 31 of the calendar year. (Wikipedia)

## Session Ten

Credit Bureau:

- A company that collects information from various sources and provides consumer credit information on individual consumers for a variety of uses. It is an organization providing information on individuals borrowing and bill paying habits. This helps lenders assess credit worthiness, the ability to pay back a loan, and can affect the interest rate and other terms of a loan. Interest rates are not the same for everyone, but instead can be based on risk-based pricing, a form of price discrimination based on the different expected risks of different borrowers, as set out in their credit rating. Consumers with poor credit repayment histories or court adjudicated debt obligations like tax liens or bankruptcies will pay a higher annual interest rate than consumers who don't have these factors. (Wikipedia)

Credit Report:

- A credit report is a record of an individual's or company's past borrowing and repaying, including information about late payments and bankruptcy. (Wikipedia)

Credit Score:

- A credit score is a numerical expression based on a statistical analysis of a person's credit files, to represent the credit worthiness of that person. A credit score is primarily based on credit report information, typically sourced from credit bureaus. Lenders, such as banks and credit card companies, use credit scores to evaluate the potential risk posed by lending money to consumers and to mitigate losses due to bad debt. Lenders use credit scores to determine who qualifies for a loan, at what interest rate, and what credit limits. Lenders also use credit scores to determine which customers are likely to bring in the most revenue. Credit scoring is not limited to banks. Other organizations, such as mobile phone companies, insurance companies, employers, landlords, and government departments employ the same techniques. (Wikipedia)

FICO score:

- The FICO score is calculated statistically, with information from a consumer's credit files. The FICO score is primarily used in credit decisions made by banks and other providers of secured and unsecured credit. It provides a snapshot of risk that banks and other institutions use to help make lending decisions. Banks may deny credit, charge higher interest rates, demand more collateral, or require extensive income and asset verification if the applicant's FICO credit score is low. Applicants with higher FICO scores may be offered better interest rates on financial instruments such as mortgages or automobile loans. (Wikipedia)

Fair Debt Collection Practices Act:

- The Fair Debt Collection Practices Act is part of the Consumer Credit Protection Act. Its purposes are to eliminate abusive practices in the collection of consumer debts, to promote fair debt collection, and to provide consumers with an avenue for disputing and obtaining validation of debt information in order to ensure the information's accuracy. It creates guidelines under which debt collectors may conduct business, defines rights of consumers involved with debt collectors, and prescribes penalties and remedies for violations. (Wikipedia)

Fair Credit Reporting Act:

- The Fair Credit Reporting Act regulates the collection, dissemination, and use of consumer information, including consumer credit information. Along with the Fair Debt Collection Practices Act, it forms the base of consumer credit rights. (Wikipedia)

Truth in Lending Act:
- A federal law designed to protect consumers. Its purpose is to promote the informed use of consumer credit by standardizing the manner in which costs associated with borrowing are calculated and disclosed. (Wikipedia)

Health Insurance:
- A form of insurance by means of which people pool the risk of incurring medical expenses. It may be provided through a government-sponsored social insurance program, or from private insurance companies. It may be purchased on a group basis (e.g., by a firm to cover its employees) or by an individual. In each case, the covered groups or individuals pay premiums or taxes to help protect themselves from unexpected healthcare expenses. (Wikipedia)

- Key health insurance terms include:
  - Premium: the amount you pay for insurance coverage.
  - Deductible: the amount per year your insurance plan requires you to pay before insurance payments kick in.
  - Co-payment: an upfront fee that your insurance requires you to pay for medical services, for example, $30 per service.
  - Co-insurance: a percentage of the overall fee that your insurance requires you to pay, for example, 20% of the price of the service

negotiated between your insurance company and the service provider.

- Exclusions: services that are not covered by the policy. You will be expected to pay the full cost of these services.
- Coverage limits: upper dollar limits on how much the insurance company will pay for either specific services, or expenses related to a time frame (annual or lifetime limits).
- If you aren't able to obtain health insurance coverage through your employer, at a minimum make sure to obtain at least a catastrophic health policy that protects you from major losses. It will be relatively inexpensive, but the insurance will only pay benefits when major expenses are incurred.

Auto Insurance:
- Insurance purchased for cars, trucks, and other vehicles. Its primary use is to provide protection against losses incurred as a result of traffic accidents and against liability that could be incurred in an accident (from Wikipedia).
- Most coverages include:
  - Bodily injury liability, an area you won't want to skimp on coverage. If you injure someone and are found liable for damages, this is the portion of your coverage that pays.
  - Property damage liability, for example $25,000 per occurrence.
  - Medical payments, for example $2,000 per person.
  - Comprehensive, relates to damage caused by non-collision situations.
  - Collision, offers protection

for damage to your car. If you drive a clunker, don't spend a lot on this.

- Uninsured/Underinsured motorist protection. (Phil Lenahan)

Renter's Insurance:

- A special type of homeowner's insurance that covers losses to personal property. (Phil Lenahan)

Identity Theft Protection:

- Identity theft is a form of fraud in which someone pretends to be someone else by assuming that person's identity, typically in order to access resources or obtain credit and other benefits in that person's name. The victim of identity theft can suffer adverse consequences if he or she is held accountable for the perpetrator's actions. (Wikipedia).

- In recent years, commercial identity theft protection/ insurance services have become available. These services purport to help protect the individual from identity theft or help detect that identity theft has occurred in exchange for a monthly or annual membership fee or premium. The services typically work either by setting fraud alerts on the individual's credit files with the three major credit bureaus or by setting up credit report monitoring with the credit bureau. While identity theft protection/insurance services have been heavily marketed, their value has been called into question. (Wikipedia)

- There are some basic practices you should follow to minimize the chances you will be a victim of identity theft, or in the event you are a victim, that you find out quickly and can take steps to reduce the impact:

- Request and review your credit report from each of the three agencies once per year (annualcreditreport.com) at four-month intervals.
- Shred sensitive information.
- Review and reconcile bank and credit card accounts.
- For the most part, you will not be held responsible for fraudulent acts done by others. However, you will be responsible for following up with creditors and other third parties to clear up issues related to identity theft. Most forms of identity theft insurance relate to assisting with the time and cost of clearing up such issues. Because you can resolve these issues on your own, identity theft insurance is more of a convenience than a must have.

Homeowner's Insurance:

- This covers private homes. It combines various personal insurance protections, which can include losses occurring to one's home, its contents, loss of its use (additional living expenses), or loss of other personal possessions of the homeowner, as well as liability insurance for accidents that may happen at the home or at the hands of the homeowner within the policy territory. (Wikipedia)
- There are several types of homeowners policies with varying levels of protection. These are labeled HO1 through HO8 and include renter's insurance (HO4). (Phil Lenahan)
- Of particular importance is making sure your policy has adequate protection for replacement cost, which

protects you for the impact that inflation has on the cost of replacing damaged property. (Phil Lenahan)

Disability Insurance:

- Insures the beneficiary's earned income against the risk that disability will make working (and therefore earning) impossible. It includes paid sick leave, short-term disability benefits, and long-term disability benefits. (Wikipedia)
- Disability insurance does not typically replace the full income of the disabled person, but rather some percentage of the earnings depending on the terms of the contract. (Phil Lenahan)
- Disability insurance is relatively expensive for the benefits received and the corresponding risks. While it is good to have some coverage,

because of the cost, it is primarily used by higher-wage professionals. (Phil Lenahan)

Life Insurance:

- A policy that pays a designated beneficiary a sum of money upon the occurrence of the insured individual's death. In return, the policy owner agrees to pay a stipulated amount at regular intervals or in lump sums. (Wikipedia)
- There are two primary forms of life insurance: permanent and temporary. Permanent forms include whole life and universal life, among others. These policies are designed to pay a benefit no matter what age a person lives to. Because a payout is expected, the cost of such insurance is high. On the other hand, temporary insurance, which is also known as "term" insurance, is

designed to pay a benefit only during a time frame chosen by the policy owner. The time frame chosen normally coincides with the time that the policyholder is at most risk—typically during the years of raising a family, often between 25 and 60 years of age. Because the probability of a payout is much less in this scenario, the cost of term insurance is correspondingly less, and is what I recommend for most families. (Phil Lenahan)

Long-Term Care:
- This type of insurance helps provide for the cost of long-term care beyond a predetermined period. It covers care generally not covered by health insurance, Medicare, or Medicaid. Individuals who require long-term care are generally not sick in the traditional sense, but instead, are unable to perform the basic activities of daily living such as dressing, bathing, eating, toileting, continence, transferring (getting in and out of a bed or chair), and walking. (Wikipedia)
- The probability is high that you will some day need assisted care as a result of physical weaknesses related to aging, so you need to prepare for that eventuality. That means either saving (self-insuring) or purchasing insurance while you are still young enough to obtain it at a reasonable cost. (Phil Lenahan)

Deductible:
- The deductible is the amount of expense that must be paid out of pocket before an insurer will cover any expenses. A general rule is the higher

the deductible, the lower the premium, and vice versa. (Wikipedia)

## Session Eleven

Tenant:

- One who pays a fee (rent) in return for the use of land, buildings, or other property owned by others. (Wiktionary)

Landlord:

- A person who owns and rents land such as a house, apartment, or condo. (Wiktionary)

Real Estate Broker/Agent:

- Real estate brokers and their salespersons (commonly called "real estate agents") assist sellers in marketing their property and selling it for the highest possible price under the best terms. When acting as a Buyer's agent with a signed agreement, they assist buyers by helping them purchase property for the lowest possible price under the best terms. Without a signed agreement, brokers may assist buyers in the acquisition of property but still represent the seller and the seller's interests. (Wikipedia)

Mortgage:

- A mortgage is a document signed by a borrower when a home loan is made that gives the lender a right to take possession of the property if the borrower fails to pay off on the loan. (HUD.gov)

Interest-Only Loan:

- A loan in which, for a set term, the borrower pays only the interest on the principal balance, with the principal balance unchanged. At the end of the interest-only term the borrower may enter an interest-only mortgage, pay the principal, or with some lenders, convert the loan to a principal and interest payment loan. (Wikipedia)

Graduated Payment Loan:

- A mortgage with low initial monthly payments that gradually increase over a specified time frame.

Negative Amortization Loan:

- Negative amortization occurs whenever the loan payment for any period is less than the interest charged over that period so that the outstanding balance of the loan increases. (Wikipedia).

Balloon Payment Loan:

- A mortgage that does not fully amortize over the term of the note, thus leaving a balance due at maturity. The final payment is called a balloon payment because of its large size. (Wikipedia)

Adjustable-Rate Loan:

- These loans, also known as variable-rate loans, usually offer a lower initial interest rate than fixed-rate loans. The interest rate fluctuates over the life of the loan based on market conditions, but the loan agreement generally sets maximum and minimum rates. When interest rates rise, generally so do your loan payments; when interest rates fall, your monthly payments may be lowered. (HUD.gov)

Fixed-Rate Loan:

- Fixed-rate loans generally have repayment terms of 15, 20, or 30 years. Both the interest rate and the monthly payments (for principal and interest) stay the same during the life of the loan. (HUD.gov)

Principal:

- The money originally invested or loaned, on which basis interest and returns are calculated. A portion of your mortgage payment goes to reduce the principal, and the rest covers interest. (Wiktionary)

Down Payment:

- A payment representing a fraction of the price of something being purchased. (Wiktionary)

Private Mortgage Insurance:

- This type of insurance protects the lender against a loss if a borrower defaults on the loan. It is usually required for loans in which the down payment is less than 20 percent of the sales price or, in a refinancing, when the amount financed is greater than 80 percent of the appraised value. (HUD.gov)

Conventional Loan:

- Mortgage loans other than those insured or guaranteed by a government agency such as the FHA (Federal Housing Administration), the VA (Veterans Administration), or the Rural Development Services (formerly known as Farmers Home Administration, or FmHA). (HUD.gov)

FHA Loan:
- A Federal Housing Administration mortgage insurance-backed mortgage loan, which are provided by FHA-approved lenders and are a type of federal assistance that has historically allowed lower-income Americans to borrow money for the purchase of a home that they would not otherwise be able to afford. A mortgage insurance premium (MIP) equal to a percentage of the loan amount at closing is required, and is normally financed by the lender and paid to FHA on the borrower's behalf. Depending on the loan-to-value ratio, there may be a monthly premium as well. (Wikipedia)

VA Loan:
- A VA loan is guaranteed by the U.S. Department of Veterans Affairs (VA). The loan may be issued by qualified lenders. The VA loan was designed to offer long-term financing to eligible American veterans. (Wikipedia)

Interest Rate:
- The cost of borrowing money expressed as a percentage rate. Interest rates can change because of market conditions. (HUD.gov)

Annual Percentage Rate:
- The cost of credit expressed as a yearly rate. The APR includes the interest rate, points, broker fees, and certain other credit charges that the borrower is required to pay. (HUD.gov)

Loan Origination Fees:
- Fees charged by the lender for processing the loan, often expressed as a percentage of the loan amount. (HUD.gov)

Points:

- Fees paid to the lender for the loan. One point equals 1 percent of the loan amount. Points are usually paid in cash at closing. In some cases, the money needed to pay points can be borrowed, but doing so increases the loan amount and the total costs. (HUD.gov)

Transaction, Settlement, or Closing Costs:

- Transaction, settlement, or closing costs may include application fees; title examination, abstract of title, title insurance, and property survey fees; fees for preparing deeds, mortgages, and settlement documents; attorneys' fees; recording fees; and notary, appraisal, and credit report fees. Under the Real Estate Settlement Procedures Act, the borrower receives a good faith estimate of closing costs at the time of application or within three days of application. The good faith estimate lists each expected cost either as an amount or a range. (HUD.gov)

Lock-In Agreement:

- A written agreement guaranteeing a home buyer a specific interest rate on a home loan provided that the loan is closed within a certain period of time, such as 60 or 90 days. Often, the agreement also specifies the number of points to be paid at closing. (HUD.gov)

Appraisal:

- A judgment or assessment of the value of something (home or property), especially a formal one. (Wiktionary)

Title:

- Legal right to ownership of a property; a deed or other certificate proving this. (Wiktionary)

Title Insurance:

- Indemnity insurance meant to protect an owner's or a lender's financial interest in real property against loss due to title defects, liens or other matters. (Wikipedia)

Escrow:

- The holding of money or documents by a neutral third party prior to closing. It can also be an account held by the lender (or servicer) into which a homeowner pays money for taxes and insurance. (HUD.gov)

Equity:

- The value of property minus liens or other encumbrances. (Wiktionary)

# Steps to Reconciling a Checkbook

**1.** Match all withdrawals and deposits on the bank statement to your check register. Use a check mark in your register to document that the item has been matched. Don't forget any of your ATM or other transactions. If, after double-checking, you find that any of your documentation doesn't match with the bank's information, call the bank.

**2.** Update your check register for any fees or other charges that you haven't recorded and that appear on your bank statement.

**3.** Bank statements provide a form for reconciling the account on the reverse side of the statement. Use that form or a software program.

**4.** Account for your deposits-in-transit by listing all deposits that appear in your checkbook that do not appear on your bank statement.

**5.** Account for your outstanding withdrawals by listing all withdrawals that appear in your checkbook that do not appear on the bank statement.

**6.** Bank statement ending balance PLUS deposits-in-transit MINUS outstanding withdrawals EQUALS checkbook balance.

**7.** If the total matches your checkbook total, then congratulations! You have successfully balanced your checkbook! If it doesn't, retrace your steps, asking yourself: Did I make an addition or subtraction error in my checkbook or my list of deposits-in-transit or outstanding withdrawals? Did I miss recording a transaction in the checkbook? (Do a quick review by check number.) Did I properly list outstanding items that carried over from the prior month's reconciliation? If after these steps you still don't reconcile, you may want to call your bank for guidance.

# Sample Résumé

**Hard Worker**

123 Main Street, Anytown, USA, 90000 · 123.456.7890 · worker@email.com

**Objective**

To obtain a position that will utilize my writing and project management skills.

**Work Experience**

Production Assistant—Wisdom Publications (2009–Present)

- Handle administrative responsibilities including status reports, accounts payable, and author contracts.
- Work with print representatives to determine and resolve all print issues.
- Recruit new vendors.
- Write back cover copy for products.
- Copyedit and proofread products.
- Improve production time and decrease costs.

Customer Service Representative—Wisdom Publications (2007–2008)

- Operated front-desk switchboard.
- Worked shifts in call center.
- Managed general customer service e-mail account.
- Performed extensive data entry involving customer accounts.
- Processed orders from call center and mailroom.
- Assisted accounts receivable department.

**Volunteer Experience**

Crisis Pregnancy Center of Red Valley (March 2008–Present)

- Take (or Receive) calls on the hotline.

St. Jane's Home for Women (June 2004–October 2007)

- Published ministry newsletter.

**Hobbies and Interests**

Reading, creative writing, hiking, cycling.

**Education**

Bachelor of Arts in Liberal Arts, Awesome College, 2004

# Form W-4

## Form W-4 (2011)

**Purpose.** Complete Form W-4 so that your employer can withhold the correct federal income tax from your pay. Consider completing a new Form W-4 each year and when your personal or financial situation changes.

**Exemption from withholding.** If you are exempt, complete **only** lines 1, 2, 3, 4, and 7 and sign the form to validate it. Your exemption for 2011 expires February 16, 2012. See Pub. 505, Tax Withholding and Estimated Tax.

**Note.** If another person can claim you as a dependent on his or her tax return, you cannot claim exemption from withholding if your income exceeds $950 and includes more than $300 of unearned income (for example, interest and dividends).

**Basic instructions.** If you are not exempt, complete the **Personal Allowances Worksheet** below. The worksheets on page 2 further adjust your withholding allowances based on itemized deductions, certain credits, adjustments to income, or two-earners/multiple jobs situations.

Complete all worksheets that apply. However, you may claim fewer (or zero) allowances. For regular wages, withholding must be based on allowances you claimed and may not be a flat amount or percentage of wages.

**Head of household.** Generally, you may claim head of household filing status on your tax return only if you are unmarried and pay more than 50% of the costs of keeping up a home for yourself and your dependent(s) or other qualifying individuals. See Pub. 501, Exemptions, Standard Deduction, and Filing Information, for information.

**Tax credits.** You can take projected tax credits into account in figuring your allowable number of withholding allowances. Credits for child or dependent care expenses and the child tax credit may be claimed using the **Personal Allowances Worksheet** below. See Pub. 919, How Do I Adjust My Tax Withholding, for information on converting your other credits into withholding allowances.

**Nonwage income.** If you have a large amount of nonwage income, such as interest or dividends, consider making estimated tax payments using Form 1040-ES, Estimated Tax for Individuals. Otherwise, you may owe additional tax. If you have pension or annuity income, see Pub. 919 to find out if you should adjust your withholding on Form W-4 or W-4P.

**Two earners or multiple jobs.** If you have a working spouse or more than one job, figure the total number of allowances you are entitled to claim on all jobs using worksheets from only one Form W-4. Your withholding usually will be most accurate when all allowances are claimed on the Form W-4 for the highest paying job and zero allowances are claimed on the others. See Pub. 919 for details.

**Nonresident alien.** If you are a nonresident alien, see Notice 1392, Supplemental Form W-4 Instructions for Nonresident Aliens, before completing this form.

**Check your withholding.** After your Form W-4 takes effect, use Pub. 919 to see how the amount you are having withheld compares to your projected total tax for 2011. See Pub. 919, especially if your earnings exceed $130,000 (Single) or $180,000 (Married).

---

### Personal Allowances Worksheet (Keep for your records.)

A   Enter "1" for **yourself** if no one else can claim you as a dependent . . . . . . . . . . . . . . . . . . . **A** _____

B   Enter "1" if:   { • You are single and have only one job; or
      • You are married, have only one job, and your spouse does not work; or   } . . . **B** _____
      • Your wages from a second job or your spouse's wages (or the total of both) are $1,500 or less.

C   Enter "1" for your **spouse**. But, you may choose to enter "-0-" if you are married and have either a working spouse or more than one job. (Entering "-0-" may help you avoid having too little tax withheld.) . . . . . . . . . **C** _____

D   Enter number of **dependents** (other than your spouse or yourself) you will claim on your tax return . . . **D** _____

E   Enter "1" if you will file as **head of household** on your tax return (see conditions under **Head of household** above) . . **E** _____

F   Enter "1" if you have at least $1,900 of **child or dependent care expenses** for which you plan to claim a credit . . . **F** _____
    (**Note.** Do **not** include child support payments. See Pub. 503, Child and Dependent Care Expenses, for details.)

G   **Child Tax Credit** (including additional child tax credit). See Pub. 972, Child Tax Credit, for more information.
    • If your total income will be less than $61,000 ($90,000 if married), enter "2" for each eligible child; then **less** "1" if you have three or more eligible children.
    • If your total income will be between $61,000 and $84,000 ($90,000 and $119,000 if married), enter "1" for each eligible child plus "1" **additional** if you have six or more eligible children . . . . . . . . . . . . . . . . **G** _____

H   Add lines A through G and enter total here. (**Note.** This may be different from the number of exemptions you claim on your tax return.) ▶ **H** _____

For accuracy, complete all worksheets that apply.
• If you plan to **itemize** or **claim adjustments to income** and want to reduce your withholding, see the **Deductions and Adjustments Worksheet** on page 2.
• If you have **more than one job** or **are married and you and your spouse both work** and the combined earnings from all jobs exceed $40,000 ($10,000 if married), see the **Two-Earners/Multiple Jobs Worksheet** on page 2 to avoid having too little tax withheld.
• If **neither** of the above situations applies, **stop here** and enter the number from line H on line 5 of Form W-4 below.

---

**Cut here and give Form W-4 to your employer. Keep the top part for your records.**

**Form W-4**
Department of the Treasury
Internal Revenue Service

## Employee's Withholding Allowance Certificate

OMB No. 1545-0074

**2011**

▶ Whether you are entitled to claim a certain number of allowances or exemption from withholding is subject to review by the IRS. Your employer may be required to send a copy of this form to the IRS.

| 1   Type or print your first name and middle initial.   Last name | 2   Your social security number |
|---|---|

Home address (number and street or rural route)

3 ☐ Single   ☐ Married   ☐ Married, but withhold at higher Single rate.
**Note.** If married, but legally separated, or spouse is a nonresident alien, check the "Single" box.

City or town, state, and ZIP code

4   If your last name differs from that shown on your social security card, check here. You must call 1-800-772-1213 for a replacement card. ▶ ☐

5   Total number of allowances you are claiming (from line **H** above **or** from the applicable worksheet on page 2)   **5** _____

6   Additional amount, if any, you want withheld from each paycheck . . . . . . . . . . . . . . **6** $ _____

7   I claim exemption from withholding for 2011, and I certify that I meet **both** of the following conditions for exemption.
    • Last year I had a right to a refund of **all** federal income tax withheld because I had **no** tax liability **and**
    • This year I expect a refund of **all** federal income tax withheld because I expect to have **no** tax liability.
    If you meet both conditions, write "Exempt" here . . . . . . . . . . . . ▶ **7** _____

Under penalties of perjury, I declare that I have examined this certificate and to the best of my knowledge and belief, it is true, correct, and complete.

**Employee's signature**
(This form is not valid unless you sign it.) ▶           Date ▶

| 8   Employer's name and address (Employer: Complete lines 8 and 10 only if sending to the IRS.) | 9   Office code (optional) | 10   Employer identification number (EIN) |
|---|---|---|

**For Privacy Act and Paperwork Reduction Act Notice, see page 2.**     Cat. No. 10220Q     Form **W-4** (2011)

# Sample Paycheck and Pay Stub

**County of Riverside**
Robert E. Byrd, CGFM, County Auditor-Controller

Pay Group: CR1-COR Biwekly 7 day FLSA   Business Unit: RIVCO
Pay Begin Date: 6/21/2007   Warrant#: 0200003834
Pay End Date: 7/04/2007   Wrnt Date: 7/18/07

**(1)**

Kris Kringle
4 Toys Avenue
North Pole CA 00001
Step Increase Date: 11/15/2008
Current Grade/Step: 154/9

Employee ID: 165215
Department: 26019532215
Location 4080 Lemon St.
Job Title: Toy Manufacturer
Pay Rate: $17.49 Hourly

| TAX DATA: | Federal | CA State |
|---|---|---|
| Marital Status: | Single | S/M-2 inc |
| Allowances: | 5 | 5 |
| Addl. Pct: | | |
| Addl. Amt: | | |

**(2)**

**(3)** HOURS AND EARNINGS

| Description | Rate | Current Hours | Current Earnings | YTD Earnings |
|---|---|---|---|---|
| Regular | 17.49 | 60.00 | 1,049.40 | 10,843.80 |
| County Overtime | 17.49 | 8.00 | 209.88 | 209.88 |
| FLSA Overtime Adjustment | | 6.00 | 104.94 | 104.94 |
| FLSA Overtime | | 2.00 | 34.98 | 34.98 |
| Holiday Used | 17.49 | 12.00 | 209.88 | 209.88 |
| Sick | 17.49 | 8.00 | 139.92 | 139.92 |
| Flexible Benefit | | | 156.25 | 1,406.25 |
| **Total:** | | 96.00 | 1,905.25 | 12,949.65 |

**(4)** TAXES

| Fed Withholdng | Current Tax | Current Tx Erns | YTD Tax | YTD Tx Erns |
|---|---|---|---|---|
| Fed Withholdng | 187.15 | 1,793.19 | 3,170.26 | 10,734.79 |
| Fed MED/EE | 26.00 | 1,793.19 | 157.53 | 11,864.11 |
| Fed OASDI/EE | 111.18 | 1,793.19 | 673.78 | 11,864.11 |
| CA Withholdng | 74.81 | 1,173.19 | 906.39 | 10,734.79 |
| **Total:** | 399.14 | | 4,907.96 | |

**(5)** BEFORE-TAX DEDUCTIONS

| Description | Current | YTD |
|---|---|---|
| Kaiser | 101.11 | 909.99 |
| Concordia Preferred | 18.48 | 166.32 |
| Medical Eye Services | 3.47 | 31.23 |
| Misc. EE Paid Retirement | 93.67 | 1,129.32 |
| **Total:** | 216.73 | 2,236.86 |

**(6)** AFTER-TAX DEDUCTIONS

| Description | Current | YTD |
|---|---|---|
| SEIU Union Dues | 6.50 | 58.50 |
| Employee Campaign | 10.00 | 150.00 |
| **Total:** | 16.50 | 208.50 |

**(7)** EMPLOYER PAID BENEFITS

| Description | Current | YTD |
|---|---|---|
| Short Term Disability* | 11.00 | 22.00 |
| *Taxable | | |

| | TOTAL GROSS | TAXABLE EARNINGS | TOTAL TAXES | TOTAL DEDUCTIONS | NET PAY |
|---|---|---|---|---|---|
| Current: | 1,905.25 | 1,793.19 | 399.14 | 233.23 | 1,272.88 |
| YTD | 12,949.65 | 10,734.19 | 4,907.96 | 2,831.85 | |

| BENE HOURS | PREV BAL | +EARNED | -USED/SOLD | +/-ADJ | CURR BAL |
|---|---|---|---|---|---|
| Vacation | 228.26 | +6.16 | | | 234.42 |
| X-Vacation | 0.00 | | | | 0.00 |
| Sick | 286.00 | +4.00 | -8.00 | | 282.00 |
| Comp | 89.90 | | | | 89.90 |
| Mgmt Comp | 0.00 | | | | 0.00 |
| Holiday | 68.00 | | -12.00 | | 56.00 |
| Admin Lve | 0.00 | | | | 0.00 |
| Annual Lve | 0.00 | | | | 0.00 |
| Personal Lve | 0.00 | | | | 0.00 |

**(8)**

NET PAY DISTRIBUTION

| Warrant #0200003834 | 1,272.88 |
|---|---|
| Total: | 1,272.88 |

**(9)**

MESSAGE:
Sign up for Direct Deposit today and join the more than 14,000 County employees currently enjoying the benefits and security of this free service!

**The County Treasurer**
of Riverside, California

County Pay Warrant
Clearing Fund

**UNION BANK OF CALIFORNIA**
Government Services Division

Warrant No.
0200003834
11-49/1210

Date: 07/18/2007          Pay Amount: $1,272.88*******

**Pay**     ****ONE THOUSAND TWO HUNDRED SEVENTY TWO AND 88/100 DOLLARS****
**To The Order Of**

V O I D

**KRIS KRINGLE**
4 Toys Avenue
North Pole, CA 00001

DIRECT DEPOSIT DISTRIBUTION

| Account Type | Account Number | Deposit Amount |
|---|---|---|
| Savings | xxxx xxxx 1234 | 250.00 |
| Checking | xxxx xxxx 2234 | 1,022.88 |
| Total: | | 1,272.88 |

**(10)**

**1.** Your employee ID will be printed here.

**2.** Income tax withholding information, including additional tax amounts that you requested be withheld from your pay are listed in this area.

**3.** All types of earnings that count as income, such as regular hours, Flexible Benefit credits, shift differentials, overtime, FLSA overtime adjustments, etc. appear here.

**4.** These are federal, state and local taxes withheld (after before-tax deductions are taken).

**5.** These are deductions taken from your earnings before taxes are calculated and withheld. These IRS defined items include before-tax contributions such as:

- Medical, dental, and optical premiums
- Flexible Spending Accounts (Health & Dependent Plans)
- Deferred compensation

**6.** Deductions taken after income taxes are calculated and withheld may include:

- Credit union deductions
- Employee Campaign contributions
- Savings bond purchase
- Supplemental life insurance
- Union/Association dues
- Van Pool deductions

**7.** Benefits your employer pays directly on your behalf may be taxable or non-taxable. Examples include:

- Long-term and short-term disability
- 401
- Vision Service Plan
- Other retirement plan options

**8.** Previous balances for leave categories are listed here along with hours earned and used. Any adjustments from prior pay periods will also be reflected, as will your new current balances.

**9.** Warrant number indicates the check number. Language may vary depending on type of organization.

**10.** A listing of bank deposits made to financial institutions for employees with Direct Deposit. Only the last four digits of the account number(s) will appear.

# Form W-2

| 22222 | **a** Employee's social security number | OMB No. 1545-0008 | | |
|---|---|---|---|---|
| **b** Employer identification number (EIN) | | | **1** Wages, tips, other compensation | **2** Federal income tax withheld |
| **c** Employer's name, address, and ZIP code | | | **3** Social security wages | **4** Social security tax withheld |
| | | | **5** Medicare wages and tips | **6** Medicare tax withheld |
| | | | **7** Social security tips | **8** Allocated tips |
| **d** Control number | | **9** | | **10** Dependent care benefits |
| **e** Employee's first name and initial  Last name  Suff. | | **11** Nonqualified plans | **12a** c o d e | |
| | | **13** Statutory employee ☐  Retirement plan ☐  Third-party sick pay ☐ | **12b** c o d e | |
| | | **14** Other | **12c** c o d e | |
| | | | **12d** c o d e | |
| **f** Employee's address and ZIP code | | | | |

| **15** State  Employer's state ID number | **16** State wages, tips, etc. | **17** State income tax | **18** Local wages, tips, etc. | **19** Local income tax | **20** Locality name |
|---|---|---|---|---|---|
| | | | | | |
| | | | | | |

Form **W-2** Wage and Tax Statement

**2011**

Department of the Treasury—Internal Revenue Service

Copy 1—For State, City, or Local Tax Department

# Sample Credit Report

Experian™
A world of insight

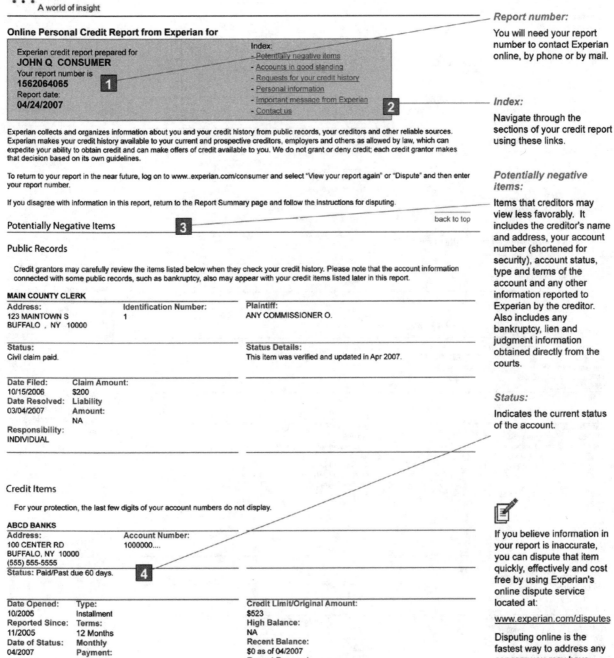

Report number:

You will need your report number to contact Experian online, by phone or by mail.

**Online Personal Credit Report from Experian for**

Experian credit report prepared for
**JOHN Q CONSUMER**
Your report number is
**1562064065**
Report date:
**04/24/2007**

**1**

Index:
- Potentially negative items
- Accounts in good standing
- Requests for your credit history
- Personal information
- Important message from Experian
- Contact us

**2**

Index:

Navigate through the sections of your credit report using these links.

Experian collects and organizes information about you and your credit history from public records, your creditors and other reliable sources. Experian makes your credit history available to your current and prospective creditors, employers and others as allowed by law, which can expedite your ability to obtain credit and can make offers of credit available to you. We do not grant or deny credit; each credit grantor makes that decision based on its own guidelines.

To return to your report in the near future, log on to www..experian.com/consumer and select "View your report again" or "Dispute" and then enter your report number.

If you disagree with information in this report, return to the Report Summary page and follow the instructions for disputing.

*Potentially negative items:*

Items that creditors may view less favorably. It includes the creditor's name and address, your account number (shortened for security), account status, type and terms of the account and any other information reported to Experian by the creditor. Also includes any bankruptcy, lien and judgment information obtained directly from the courts.

## Potentially Negative Items    **3**    back to top

## Public Records

Credit grantors may carefully review the items listed below when they check your credit history. Please note that the account information connected with some public records, such as bankruptcy, also may appear with your credit items listed later in this report.

**MAIN COUNTY CLERK**

| Address: | Identification Number: | Plaintiff: |
|---|---|---|
| 123 MAINTOWN S | 1 | ANY COMMISSIONER O. |
| BUFFALO , NY  10000 | | |

| Status: | | Status Details: |
|---|---|---|
| Civil claim paid. | | This item was verified and updated in Apr 2007. |

| Date Filed: | Claim Amount: |
|---|---|
| 10/15/2006 | $200 |
| Date Resolved: | Liability |
| 03/04/2007 | Amount: |
| | NA |
| Responsibility: | |
| INDIVIDUAL | |

*Status:*

Indicates the current status of the account.

## Credit Items

For your protection, the last few digits of your account numbers do not display.

**ABCD BANKS**

| Address: | Account Number: |
|---|---|
| 100 CENTER RD | 1000000.... |
| BUFFALO, NY  10000 | |
| (555) 555-5555 | |
| Status: Paid/Past due 60 days.  **4** | |

| Date Opened: | Type: | Credit Limit/Original Amount: |
|---|---|---|
| 10/2005 | Installment | $523 |
| Reported Since: | Terms: | High Balance: |
| 11/2005 | 12 Months | NA |
| Date of Status: | Monthly | Recent Balance: |
| 04/2007 | Payment: | $0 as of 04/2007 |
| | $0 | Recent Payment: |
| Last Reported: | Responsibility: | $0 |
| 04/2007 | Individual | |

If you believe information in your report is inaccurate, you can dispute that item quickly, effectively and cost free by using Experian's online dispute service located at:

www.experian.com/disputes

Disputing online is the fastest way to address any concern you may have about the information in your credit report.

Account History:
60 days as of 12-2006
30 days as of 11-2006

**MAIN COLL AGENCIES**

| Address: | Account Number: | Original Creditor: |
|---|---|---|
| PO BOX 123 | 0123456789 | TELEVISE CABLE COMM. |
| ANYTOWN, PA 10000 | | |
| (555) 555-5555 | | |

Status: Collection account. $95 past due as of 4-2000.

| Date Opened: | Type: | Credit Limit/Original Amount: |
|---|---|---|
| 01/2005 | Installment | $95 |
| Reported Since: | Terms: | High Balance: |
| 04/2005 | NA | NA |
| Date of Status: | Monthly | Recent Balance: |
| 04/2005 | Payment: | $95 as of 04/2005 |
| | $0 | Recent Payment: |
| Last Reported: | Responsibility: | $0 |
| 04/2005 | Individual | |

Your statement:  ITEM DISPUTED BY CONSUMER

Account History:
Collection as of 4-2005

Accounts in Good Standing                          **5**                          back to top

**AUTOMOBILE AUTO FINANCE**

| Address: | Account Number: |
|---|---|
| 100 MAIN ST E | 12345678998.... |
| SMALLTOWN, MD 90001 | |
| (555) 555-5555 | |

Status: Open/Never late.

| Date Opened: | Type: **6** | Credit Limit/Original Amount: |
|---|---|---|
| 01/2006 | Installment | $10,355 |
| Reported Since: | Terms: | High Balance: |
| 01/2006 | 65 Months | NA |
| Date of Status: | Monthly | Recent Balance: |
| 04/2007 | Payment: | $7,984 as of 04/2007 |
| | $210 | Recent Payment: |
| Last Reported: | Responsibility: | $0 |
| 04/2007 | Individual | |

**MAIN**

| Address: | Account Number: |
|---|---|
| PO BOX 1234 | 1234567899876 |
| FORT LAUDERDALE, FL 10009 | |

Status: Closed/Never late.

| Date Opened: | Type: | Credit Limit/Original Amount: |
|---|---|---|
| 03/1997 | Revolving | NA |
| Reported Since: | Terms: | High Balance: |
| 03/1997 | 1 Months | $3,228 |
| Date of Status: | Monthly | Recent Balance: |
| 08/2006 | Payment: | $0 /paid as of 08/2006 |
| | $0 | Recent Payment: |
| Last Reported: | Responsibility: | $0 |
| 08/2006 | Individual | |

Your statement:
Account closed at consumer's request

*Accounts in good standing:*

**Lists accounts that have a positive status and may be viewed favorably by creditors. Some creditors do not report to us, so some of your accounts may not be listed.**

*Type:*

Account type indicates whether your account is a revolving or an installment account.

Requests for Your Credit History   back to top

### Requests Viewed By Others

We make your credit history available to your current and prospective creditors and employers as allowed by law. Personal data about you may be made available to companies whose products and services may interest you.

The section below lists all who have requested in the recent past to review your credit history as a result of actions involving you, such as the completion of a credit application or the transfer of an account to a collection agency, application for insurance, mortgage or loan application, etc. Creditors may view these requests when evaluating your creditworthiness.

#### HOMESALE REALTY CO

| Address: | Date of Request: |
|---|---|
| 2000 S MAINROAD BLVD STE | 07/16/2006 |
| ANYTOWN CA 11111 | |
| (555) 555-5555 | |

Comments:
Real estate loan on behalf of 3903 MERCHANTS EXPRESS M. This inquiry is scheduled to continue on record until 8-2008.

#### M & T BANK

| Address: | Date of Request: |
|---|---|
| PO BOX 100 | 02/23/2006 |
| BUFFALO NY 10000 | |
| (555) 555-5555 | |

Comments:
Permissible purpose. This inquiry is scheduled to continue on record until 3-2008.

#### WESTERN FUNDING INC

| Address: | Date of Request: |
|---|---|
| 191 W MAIN AVE STE 100 | 01/25/2006 |
| INTOWN CA 10000 | |
| (559) 555-5555 | |

Comments:
Permissible purpose. This inquiry is scheduled to continue on record until 2-2008.

### Requests Viewed Only By You

The section below lists all who have a permissible purpose by law and have requested in the recent past to review your information. You may not have initiated these requests, so you may not recognize each source. We offer information about you to those with a permissible purpose, for example, to:

- other creditors who want to offer you preapproved credit;
- an employer who wishes to extend an offer of employment;
- a potential investor in assessing the risk of a current obligation;
- Experian or other credit reporting agencies to process a report for you;
- your existing creditors to monitor your credit activity (date listed may reflect only the most recent request).

We report these requests **only to you** as a record of activities. We **do not** provide this information to other creditors who evaluate your creditworthiness.

#### MAIN BANK USA

| Address: | Date of Request: |
|---|---|
| 1 MAIN CTR AA 11 | 08/10/2006 |
| BUFFALO NY 14203 | |

#### MYTOWN BANK

| Address: | Date of Request: |
|---|---|
| PO BOX 825 | 08/05/2006 |
| MYTOWN DE 10000 | |
| (555) 555-5555 | |

#### INTOWN DATA CORPS

| Address: | Date of Request: |
|---|---|
| 2000 S MAINTOWN BLVD STE | 07/16/2006 |
| INTOWN CO 11111 | |
| (555) 555-5555 | |

---

*Requests for your credit history:*

Also called "inquiries," requests for your credit history are logged on your report whenever anyone reviews your credit information. There are two types of inquiries.

i.
Inquiries resulting from a transaction initiated by you. These include inquiries from your applications for credit, insurance, housing or other loans. They also include transfer of an account to a collection agency. Creditors may view these items when evaluating your creditworthiness.

ii.
Inquiries resulting from transactions you may not have initiated but that are allowed under the FCRA. These include preapproved offers, as well as for employment, investment review, account monitoring by existing creditors, and requests by you for your own report. These items are shown only to you and have no impact on your creditworthiness or risk scores.

## Personal Information 〔8〕

**Names:**
JOHN Q CONSUMER
Name identification number: 15621

JONATHON Q CONSUMER
Name identification number: 15622

J Q CONSUMER
Name identification number: 15623

**Social Security number variations:**
999999999

**Year of birth:**
1959

**Spouse or co-applicant:**
JANE

**Employers:**
ABCDE ENGINEERING CORP

**Telephone numbers:**
(555) 555 5555 Residential

**Address:** 123 MAIN STREET
ANYTOWN, MD 90001-9999
**Address identification number:**
0277741504
**Type of Residence:** Multifamily
**Geographical Code:** 0-156510-31-8840

**Address:** 555 SIMPLE PLACE
ANYTOWN, MD 90002-7777
**Address identification number:**
0170086050
**Type of Residence:** Single family
**Geographical Code:** 0-176510-33-8840

〔9〕

**Address:** 999 HIGH DRIVE APT 15B
ANYTOWN, MD 90003-5555
**Address identification number:**
0170129301
**Type of Residence:** Apartment complex
**Geographical Code:** 0-156510-31-8840

*Personal information:*

Personal information associated with your history that has been reported to Experian by you, your creditors and other sources.

May include name and Social Security number variations, employers, telephone numbers, etc. Experian lists all variations so you know what is being reported to us as belonging to you.

*Address information:*

Your current address and previous address(es)

## Your Personal Statement 〔10〕

No general personal statements appear on your report.

*Personal statement:*

Any personal statement that you added to your report appears here.

Note - statements remain as part of the report for two years and display to anyone who has permission to review your report.

## Important Message From Experian                    back to top

## Contacting Us                    back to top

Contact address and phone number for your area will display here.

# Mortgage Shopping Worksheet

| | Lender 1 | | Lender 2 | |
|---|---|---|---|---|
| | mortgage 1 | mortgage 2 | mortgage 1 | mortgage 2 |
| **Name of Lender:** ............................... | | | | |
| **Name of Contact:** .............................. | | | | |
| **Date of Contact:** ............................... | | | | |
| **Mortgage Amount:** ............................. | | | | |

## Basic Information on the Loans

| | mortgage 1 | mortgage 2 | mortgage 1 | mortgage 2 |
|---|---|---|---|---|
| Type of Mortgage: fixed rate, adjustable rate, conventional, FHA, other? If adjustable, see below .............. | | | | |
| Minimum down payment required ................... | | | | |
| Loan term (length of loan) ........................ | | | | |
| Contract interest rate ............................ | | | | |
| Annual percentage rate (APR) .................... | | | | |
| Points (may be called loan discount points) .......... | | | | |
| Monthly Private Mortgage Insurance (PMI) premiums .... | | | | |
| How long must you keep PMI? .................... | | | | |
| Estimated monthly **escrow** for taxes and hazard insurance | | | | |
| Estimated monthly payment (Principal, Interest, Taxes, Insurance, PMI) ............................. | | | | |

## Fees

Different institutions may have different names for some fees and may charge different fees. We have listed some typical fees you may see on loan documents.

| | mortgage 1 | mortgage 2 | mortgage 1 | mortgage 2 |
|---|---|---|---|---|
| Application fee or Loan processing fee ............... | | | | |
| Origination fee or Underwriting fee ................. | | | | |
| Lender fee or Funding fee......................... | | | | |
| Appraisal fee .................................... | | | | |
| Attorney fees.................................... | | | | |
| Document preparation and recording fees ............. | | | | |
| Broker fees (may be quoted as points, origination fees, or interest rate add-on)........................ | | | | |
| Credit report fee ................................ | | | | |
| Other fees...................................... | | | | |

## Other Costs at Closing/Settlement

| | mortgage 1 | mortgage 2 | mortgage 1 | mortgage 2 |
|---|---|---|---|---|
| Title search/Title insurance | | | | |
| For lender................................... | | | | |
| For you .................................... | | | | |
| Estimated prepaid amounts for interest, taxes, hazard insurance, payments to escrow ............ | | | | |
| State and local taxes, stamp taxes, transfer taxes ....... | | | | |
| Flood determination ............................. | | | | |
| Prepaid Private Mortgage Insurance (PMI)............. | | | | |
| Surveys and home inspections ..................... | | | | |
| **Total Fees and Other Closing/Settlement Cost Estimates** ................................. | | | | |

| | Lender 1 | | Lender 2 | |
|---|---|---|---|---|
| **Name of Lender:** ............................... | | | | |
| | mortgage 1 | mortgage 2 | mortgage 1 | mortgage 2 |
| **Other Questions and Considerations about the Loan** | | | | |
| Are any of the fees or costs waivable? ............... | | | | |
| **Prepayment penalties** | | | | |
| Is there a prepayment penalty? .................... | | | | |
| If so, how much is it? ......................... | | | | |
| How long does the penalty period last? (for example, 3 years? 5 years?) ......................... | | | | |
| Are extra principal payments allowed? ............... | | | | |
| **Lock-ins** | | | | |
| Is the lock-in agreement in writing? ................ | | | | |
| Is there a fee to lock-in? ........................ | | | | |
| When does the lock-in occur—at application, approval, or another time? ..................... | | | | |
| How long will the lock-in last? .................... | | | | |
| If the rate drops before closing, can you lock-in at a lower rate? ............................. | | | | |
| **If the loan is an adjustable rate mortgage:** | | | | |
| What is the initial rate? ......................... | | | | |
| What is the maximum the rate could be next year? ...... | | | | |
| What are the rate and payment caps each year and over the life of the loan? ..................... | | | | |
| What is the frequency of rate change and of any changes to the monthly payment? ................ | | | | |
| What is the index that the lender will use? ............ | | | | |
| What margin will the lender add to the index? ......... | | | | |
| **Credit life insurance** | | | | |
| Does the monthly amount quoted to you include a charge for credit life insurance? ............... | | | | |
| If so, does the lender require credit life insurance as a condition of the loan? .................... | | | | |
| How much does the credit life insurance cost? ......... | | | | |
| How much lower would your monthly payment be without the credit life insurance? ................ | | | | |
| If the lender does not require credit life insurance, and you still want to buy it, what rates can you get from other insurance providers? ................ | | | | |

# Resources from Veritas Financial Ministries

## GOD'S WAY TO FINANCIAL FREEDOM

### Phil's E-Letter (FREE)

Sign up to receive Phil's free monthly E-Letter. Packed with timely and invaluable guidance to help you better manage your money.

### Life and Money Radio

Listen as Phil addresses important financial issues of the day and answers callers' questions.

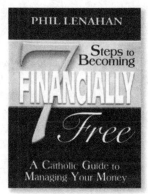

### 7 Steps to Becoming Financially Free

Learn step-by-step how to achieve true financial freedom. Available for individual and small group study.

### Generation Next

The program that will revolutionize young people's attitudes and actions with money. For ages 17-25.

### Parish Bulletin Article Program

Bring Phil's common-sense, Catholic-based teaching directly to parishioners through your parish bulletin.

### Seminars and Online Classes

- Learn the principles of financial freedom directly from Phil by attending his online classes.
- Invite Phil to speak at your parish or Catholic conference.

Visit veritasfinancialministries.com to learn more about these and other resources to help you be truly financially free!

# VERITAS
## FINANCIAL MINISTRIES